"Is there any woman anywhere who does̶n̶ ̶ ̶ ̶ ̶ ̶ ̶ ̶ ̶ ̶ ̶ ̶ ̶ ̶ significance? Her purpose? *Beautiful Warrior* helps biblically equip women to overcome some of those blasted insecurities that can get in the way of a fruitful life. Getting the focus off a cockeyed self-esteem and getting a 20/20 handle on God esteem? Oh, man. This is going to make all the difference!"

—Rhonda Rhea, TV personality, humor columnist,
and author of fourteen books, including *Messy to Meaningful,*
Fix Her Upper, and the award-winning *Turtles in the Road*

"The fresh, clear voice of Tina Yeager beautifully reminds us to strip away the lies we've allowed to mar our identity so we can finally grasp who God says we are: heroines of the faith."

—Linda Evans Shepherd, author of *Praying God's Promises*
and *When You Need to Move a Mountain*

"Tina Yeager's book *Beautiful Warrior* is a must-read for any woman who has ever struggled with insecurity or self-doubt. Her raw transparency is refreshing as she shares her personal struggles of knowing her self-worth and believing she's good enough. Tina lets you know we're all in this battle together, calling us 'sister warriors,' as we war against low self-esteem and the constant need for approval. I only wish I'd had this book in my hands twenty years ago. It's a game changer."

—Michelle Medlock Adams, bestselling,
award-winning author of more than eighty books

"I dearly love *Beautiful Warrior.* This book is a must-read for those of us who desperately want to ditch our defeating low self-esteem and instead be uplifted by Christ-esteem. You'll learn practical, doable techniques for empowerment to change your own status and become the incredible woman God created you to be. An excellent read for groups as well as individuals."

—Debora M. Coty, award-winning author of more than forty inspirational books,
including the bestselling Too Blessed to Be Stressed series

"If you've ever struggled with insecurity, unhealthy comparisons, suffocating fears, or self-defeating thoughts, *Beautiful Warrior* is your advanced ticket to victory. Tina Yeager offers her expertise as a licensed therapist *and* extends the voice of a trusted friend who understands the fight from within. She gives clear-cut solutions to expose, confront, and conquer every woman's emotional battles. It's a must-read!"

—Leah DiPascal, writer, speaker, and Bible teacher

"Tina Yeager writes powerfully and intimately, as if giving each reader her undivided attention. Tapping into the core struggle women of all ages face, Tina helps readers evade the inevitable pitfalls low self-esteem causes while offering practical tools for individual healing and wholeness. Using her wisdom as a skilled professional counselor pared with guidance from God's Holy Word, this book is packed with power that will surely transform lives for the better. *Beautiful Warrior* is a must-read for women of all ages. It's an honor to endorse a book holding so much potential."

—LaTan Roland Murphy, author, featured columnist,
event speaker, and vocalist

"*Beautiful Warrior* struck chords in me I didn't know existed, teaching me so much about myself . . . the way I see myself . . . and the difference in that and how God sees me. Tina Yeager has drawn from a deep, deep well of emotion and truth to remind us who we are at the core of ourselves: daughters of the King."

—Eva Marie Everson, best-selling author and speaker,
president, Word Weavers International

"As a professional speaker and writer, I see women allowing themselves to be attacked with lies, self-doubt, low self-esteem, and all the other issues that follow. *Beautiful Warrior* offers skills to become our own heroines and be the women God created us to be."

—Jane Jenkins Herlong, CSP, CPAE, award-winning and bestselling
author of *Bury Me with My Pearls* and *Rhinestones on My Flip-Flops*

"With raw vulnerability, Tina Yeager takes you on a journey of self-discovery that leads you to not only know yourself better but, most importantly, understand the God who finds you absolutely lovable."

—Bethany Jett, award-winning author and owner of Serious Writer Inc.

"Self-esteem is a tricky thing—and healthy self-esteem even more so. Everywhere we turn someone has a new version of what this should look like. Tina Yeager has drilled down to the core of biblical truth and given us a blueprint for building a healthy self-image. Her insight and wisdom are delivered with candid transparency and kindness. This is truly a book for everyone."

—Edie Melson, award-winning author and director
of the Blue Ridge Mountains Christian Writers Conference

"With the talent of a gifted writer, the knowledge of a licensed therapist, and the experience of an overcomer, Tina Yeager's words are therapeutic and life-changing. Her word tapestry is both challenging and healing. If you're tired of fighting insecurity, comparison, and approval addiction, you need this book. Many of us need *Beautiful Warrior* to find the warrior inside our hearts. She's there. Let Tina help you find her."

—Andy Lee, author of *A Mary Like Me: Flawed Yet Called*

TINA YEAGER

BEAUTIFUL WARRIOR

*Finding Victory Over the Lies
Formed Against You*

NEW HOPE
PUBLISHERS
Imprint of Iron Stream Media

BIRMINGHAM, ALABAMA

New Hope® Publishers
5184 Caldwell Mill Rd.
St. 204-221
Hoover, AL 35244
NewHopePublishers.com
An imprint of Iron Stream Media
IronStreamMedia.com

Library of Congress Cataloging-in-Publication Data

Names: Yeager, Tina, author.
Title: Beautiful warrior : finding victory over the lies formed against you /
   Tina Yeager.
Description: First [edition]. | Birmingham : New Hope Publishers, 2019.
Identifiers: LCCN 2019008893 | ISBN 9781563092305 (permabind)
Subjects: LCSH: Christian women—Religious life. | Truthfulness and
   falsehood—Religious aspects—Christianity. | Identity
   (Psychology)—Religious aspects—Christianity.
Classification: LCC BV4527 .Y43 2019 | DDC 248.8/43—dc23
LC record available at https://lccn.loc.gov/2019008893

ISBN-13: 978-1-56309-230-5
Ebook ISBN: 978-1-56309-153-7

1 2 3 4 5—23 22 21 20 19

This book is dedicated to my Savior and the warrior tribe
He sent to encourage me when I struggled to believe in my purpose.
Thank You for breathing hope into my wings.

CONTENTS

CONTENTS

P lease allow me to acknowledge the saints and warrior friends who made this book possible.

Of course, the Lord deserves my utmost thanks. "You are worthy, our Lord and God, to receive glory and honor and power, for you created all things, and by your will they were created and have their being" (Revelation 4:11).

My husband Tyler has my love and appreciation forever. Thank you for believing in my purpose and remaining such a valiant and chivalrous hero at my side each day.

I owe immense gratitude to Eva Marie Everson. Without her support and masterful editing, this book would have remained unpublishable. Moreover, her leadership of Word Weavers International granted me membership in a writing family.

Heartfelt thanks to my Christ-sisters, Jan Powell, Donna Mumma, and Michelle Whitman. Your encouragement and prayer support means more than you'll ever know.

I must offer profound appreciation to my amazing agent Julie Gwinn, whose diligence and expertise carried me across the publishing threshold. Thank you for your faithfulness in championing my work.

Many thanks to Ramona Richards, Reagan Jackson, Tina Atchenson, and all those at Iron Stream Media and New Hope Publishers whose faithful work crafted my manuscript into a book.

I'm particularly grateful for each reader who invested time in the *Beautiful Warrior* message. May the Holy Spirit anoint each word as a blessing to your soul.

WHY ME?

F resh print lured me in. Textured hardcovers called for me to caress them. Smooth pages kissed my fingertips. Written treasures dazzled my eyes as I floated along the aisles. Book-intoxicated passion drew me further.

Dead center in the bookstore, I froze. Dread raised the hair on my arms. I tried to dismiss the foreboding. Told myself to keep moving. Shake it off. As though ignoring the trigger could prevent the inevitable attack. But it was too late now.

I had ventured into a known battleground. I recognized the incoming assault. Familiar doubts shot through my head. Repercussions shook my core and sent tremors into my soles.

Look at all these books on the clearance table.

I swallowed hard. Stiffened. Prepared for inbound missiles, the ones that always came next.

If there are so many books already on clearance, who needs your words? Thousands of acclaimed experts fill these aisles with advice. Who do you think you are?

Celebrities beamed from book jackets lining the shelves around me. The experts seemed to sneer from those photos. I lowered my gaze to the carpet. I could hear the subsequent bombs heading toward me, even before the words made a full impact.

You're nobody. Just give up.

I steeled myself. The crash of self-doubt and despair had stung tears into my eyes in the past. After fighting this war for so many years, would I lose another battle here in the bookstore?

I considered the carpet in front of me. A billion loops of hardy fiber massed together. Designed for heavy traffic. Though stained and worn, it supported countless soles. Multitudes wandered this battleground. How many others would the enemy crush with these missiles of doubt and despair?

I clenched my fists. No self-pitying tears this time. This attack deserved a warrior's response. I narrowed my eyes. For once, I raged at the lie instead of myself. Called the enemy for what it was—a low-bellied reptile. The uncreative, oldest of bullies. Then I commissioned the ultimate defense—truth's iron dome.

Nobody? There's no one here by that name. My identity comes from a higher authority than yours. Not to mention that I wasn't called to give up.

I lifted my gaze to the books lining my pathway. Space remained at the edges of the top shelves, enough to accommodate future releases. I scanned the cover photos and the aisles full of customers—none of them were named Nobody. All these people had significance. If I had a chance to help one other person survive this battle, I had to persevere in my call to write.

But the enemy persisted in his attacks. I faced many temptations to quit, especially during the course of writing this book. Yet despite many challenges and rewrites, I got up from each painful blow, determined to fight through these pages.

An authority higher than mine had called me. The process taught and strengthened me. I forged onward in devotion to the ultimate healer. My *true* source of identity. In days riddled with doubt, the loving call of Christ willed me onward, reminding me that he had given up everything to redefine me. And not only me; the healer offers new identity to everyone.

Which is why I often thought of you. Esteem attacks may not happen to you in bookshops. Perhaps discouragement targets you in clothing stores, at work, or even at home. But while the doubts ambush you in different locations from mine, we still face the same enemy. His ancient strategy shows little deviation. He strikes tender spots. Attacks purpose. Draws the victim in as his accomplice.

My hope is that my sacrifice on this battlefield saves you from a bullet of self-defeat, but if you're expecting me to have it all together, I will most certainly disappoint you. I have yet to declare victory. But I *do* stop the bully when I stop fighting against myself. When I refuse to take these attacks lying down.

So, then let us learn to stand together as sister warriors. We are created with divine strength. Our natural ferocity must not be wasted on self-enmity. Nor should we fear one another from a position of insecurity. None of us may have it *all* together, but we can face it all if we *stand* together in our divine calling and strength.

Chapter 1

HELLO, MY NAME *ISN'T*

I bent over the spiritual retreat's sign-in table, permanent marker poised over the "hello my name is" sticker. I hesitated, struggling to decide what to reveal on this label without exposing too much.

I had not come to offer psychotherapy services. I wouldn't need to add the LMHC (licensed mental health counselor) title at the end. A surname would distinguish me as the "Tina married to Mr. Yeager." I could safely write my last name without sharing too much about myself. Those who recognized my face would identify me by a four-letter label.

Tina, the "Christ-follower" by definition, had been chosen for the "Name Given" box on my birth certificate by parents not yet acquainted with my character. While my tiny, raw fists pounded against an uncertain enemy. While I screamed to protest my own breath.

Since birth, people have seen only the surface of who I really am. My mask. They call me by the cheerful name on my papers. Conditioned, I responded to Tina and hid any doubts. In secret, I called myself by other names instead. Less friendly four-letter words. The type of slander one reserves for an enemy.

Those titles could never be shared, especially on a badge, so I wrote, "Tina Yeager." I fitted my mask to face the greeters and offered the Christ-follower smile they expected from me.

I strode into the dormitory, confident my mask would hold secure. The façade had never failed to cover all my battle scars. Besides, I reasoned, attending as a participant instead of faculty ought to prove easy. At a church event where I had no responsibilities, I expected my best people-pleasing behavior to shine. Calm ought to grace my every move and scent the wake of my path.

By the middle of the weekend, something raw and messy surged forth. If only the retreat had limited itself to a superficial theme, my veneer might have survived. But the message plunged a crowbar into a shadowy compartment of my heart. A triggered nerve vaulted my darkest insecurities to the surface, and my serene persona shattered.

I never felt so resistant, so compelled to rebel against words and events. Snark and sarcasm burgeoned forth. Complaints spurted at those around me and leaders about songs, food . . . everything. I even converted my water bottle into a squirt gun, blasting the volunteers who woke us.

Yes. I really did.

I assumed the mood would pass. I thought my inner strife would end at some point and I could reposition my nice-girl mask. Instead, the tension worsened. My attitude soured as the discussions built toward their climax. Though I didn't recognize *why* I changed, an unconscious part of my mind dug its heels into the threshold it guarded. I could not *allow* this prying to expose me.

As the chaplain concluded the weekend's pivotal message, volunteers carried white loaves into the audience. If they served as part of a communion ritual, I might have endured the experience better. But these bite-sized bits weren't for eating. The bread represented a spiritual issue. The chaplain invited us to surrender our symbolic burdens at the altar cross. This dying moment, he promised, offered a chance to rise anew.

"My wife and I will be available to pray with anyone who needs it," Reverend Hall said, then took a seat in the audience.

I shifted on the pew's thin pad and glared into my cupped hands. The pinched morsel of bread seemed to weigh five pounds.

I was *not* going to cry.

Footsteps swept past me, but I sat rigid.

Other women might need the pastor's time. Let him and his wife pray with them. Not me. I was fine.

Like always.

The back door clicked open and shut several times. I glanced up at women breezing down the aisle to lay their burdens in the basket by the cross.

I swallowed a stubborn clench stuck in my throat and resumed my downward focus as breadcrumbs melted into pasty drops on my palms. Maybe, I thought, the burden would stick forever in my dewy grasp.

Reverend Hall called my name.

I raised my heavy chin and scanned the room, as though someone else by the same name lingered there. The others had gone, and I remained the sole participant in the chapel.

Reverend Hall and his wife settled into the nearest pew and torqued the crowbar. "Can we pray with you?"

Broken, like the bread, I sobbed out a stream of long-buried insecurities. Their dark theme emerged to expose the name badge I'd always scrawled on the inner walls of my identity: UNLOVABLE.

My inner guard collapsed and my fight dropped to its knees. Exhausted to the core, I sat covered in the mess of my ugly cry. I had *heard* the message all weekend, but now I sat ready to *listen*. My knees cracked when I rose and approached the chapel railing. I faced the cross. A feature gleamed there, one I hadn't noticed in hundreds of prayers and worship services before this one—identity.

I dropped the bread into the basket along with my self-made names, both the veneer and the burden. I knew the shift would demand more than pasty crumb-droppings. Engraving a new name on my soul would require gut-wrenching work. But I committed myself to the effort in this first step. My true identity—I finally understood—must come from Christ.

I wish I could say my insecurities vanished in that moment. Years of attacks from the enemy and myself had etched slanderous scars on the inner walls of my heart.

Foolish. Waste. Mess. Pathetic. Failure. Worthless. Unlovable. And on and on . . .

I had to scour away the lies and rewrite Christ's new name within my self-concept. His redeemed identity for me had been true since the dawn of our relationship, but I needed to work at accepting it.

The choice to begin building my esteem on Christ marked the first step in this long journey. The good news was I didn't have to endure it on my own strength, even though the battle often tempted me to believe I was alone.

Conditioning tempts us to adopt an identity based upon others' judgments, circumstances, or the record of our mistakes. But the sum of things past and present fall short of *God's* perspective, including how He defines us. Unlike the guesses made by our parents at birth, He names us according to inert potential we can only fulfill when united with His Spirit.

Four-letter slurs can continue to limit us as long as we believe in them instead. Whatever names rise in puckered scar tissue from our hearts, our Creator knows our true essence as he dreamed it: "For he chose us in him before the creation of the world to be holy and blameless in his sight. In love he predestined us for adoption" (Ephesians 1:4–5).

Scripture abounds with examples of God redefining His servants before they showed any sign of living up to their new name. He called Gideon a "mighty warrior" (Judges 6:12) while he cowered in a winepress. He renamed Abram, which means, "exalted father," to Abraham, which means, "father of many" (Genesis 17:5), even while the old man and his wife remained childless. The Lord defined Moses as the deliverer of his people when the stuttering murderer lacked the character needed to fulfill his role and begged God to find someone else.

Jesus renamed Simon as Peter, the "rock" upon which His church would be built (Matthew 16:18). Yet this disciple's great insecurity would soon lead him to deny Christ. Like the patriarchs before him, Simon Peter still needed work before he reflected the identity foretold by the Lord.

Engraved markings and deep gouges take backbreaking effort to remove. Fortunately, God provides the muscle to buff out our old nature. It isn't all up to us.

Jesus didn't leave Simon to transform into a rock on his own strength. But the would-be apostle had to participate in the process. As in all biblical and modern-day examples, he offered the disciple a personal experience to renew his identity. The Lord strolled alongside Simon Peter and other spiritual forerunners then and still comes to walk with us today. Christ authors our significance and cultivates us toward fulfilling our divine identity—not a transient name dependent on our own effort but one stitched into our DNA by the indwelling Spirit of our Creator.

The Lord values our identity so much he engraved our names on His hands (Isaiah 49:16). Christ includes our divine identity in His loving outreach as an indelible component of each thing He touches. Our potential, our true value, rides upon the scarred palms of the Lord.

We march onto the battlefield against evil in *His* truth and grace. The Lord reveals Himself in Scripture by his own names, one being *Jehovah Nissi*, which means "The Lord our banner" (Exodus 17:15; Song of Songs 2:4; Isaiah 11:10–12). *Jehovah Nissi* is the battle standard he raises over us as we march onward. Our significance rests not within our circumstances but *in the standard and identity under which we engage.*

The Lord our Banner gathers our names to himself. Therefore, our fellow servants' names weave together with our own on the standard flying overhead.

Sisters at my side, with Christ over us, let us not be tricked into believing we fight the wars within on our own. Children of the King need not stand alone on this or any other front.

While many of us *struggle* with self-esteem, others remain unaware of our common plight because we guard the secret so well. We hide in public behind our kept-together masks. We label ourselves as "fine" instead of "struggling," as though "fine" serves as a password admitting us to society.

If someone asks, "How are you?" we snap the acceptable reply, and redirect the focus. "Fine. How are *you*?"

An honest response could cause enough shock to unsettle our masks, and we simply can't take that chance.

But we're not fine. Nearly one in ten American women suffers from clinical depression and countless others experience the symptoms at nonclinical levels.[1] Fifty-eight percent of adults in the US report stress related to their relationships and responsibilities.[2]

Low self-esteem grows with us, it seems. According to a global study, 62 percent of girls report feeling insecure while 96 percent of women worldwide do not consider themselves beautiful.[3] The statistics paint a picture of millions in distress, but none of us want to open our hearts to share the truth. Instead, we grit our teeth and smile.

---

1. Laura A. Pratt, Ph.D., and Debra J. Brody, M.P.H., "Depression in the U.S. Household Population, 2009-2012," NCHS Data Brief No. 172, December 2014, CDC, https://www.cdc .gov/nchs/data/databriefs/db172.htm.
2. "The Impact of Stress," American Psychological Association, accessed October 25, 2018, http://www.apa.org/news/press/releases/stress/2011/impact.aspx.
3. "The Dove Self Esteem Project," Dove, accessed October 25, 2018, https://www.dove .com/us/en/stories/about-dove/our-vision.html.

The threat of exposure drives a chill deeper into the marrow than the most harrowing nightmare. No one must know who we truly are because we're certain they won't accept us.

Mostly because we don't accept ourselves.

If anyone saw the vulnerable depths of our souls, their judgment would cause unbearable pain. We assume others would respond to us with the same disdain we harbor against ourselves.

We're. Not. Fine. By pretending we are, we block the sincere relationships that would shatter our loneliness and launch us toward healing. We can't get out of this quicksand of self-abasement unless we reach out. But in order to reach out, we have to realize others are close enough to our situation to merely wiggle their fingers to take hold of our hands.

The fairytale princess of the 1980s and 90s, Diana, Princess of Wales, epitomized the loneliness of secret pain, and she may never have fully understood the global impact of her story. Despite popularity and status, "Princess Di" suffered from bulimia and depression. Her husband's pursuit of a former girlfriend identified her as the unloved, second choice.

In an interview with BBC in 1995, only two years before her untimely death, the most adored celebrity of her time revealed her self-perception as she wed the prince by saying, "As far as I was concerned I was a fat, chubby, twenty-year-old, twenty-one-year-old, and I couldn't understand the level of interest."[4] A biography by Andrew Morton in 1992 publicized her emotional struggles, exposing women throughout the world to the fact that they were not alone.[5]

----

4. "The Panorama Interview," BBC News, accessed April 9, 2019, http://www.bbc.co.uk/news/special/politics97/diana/panorama.html#top.

5. Andrew Morton, *Diana: Her True Story—In Her Own Words* (New York: Simon and Schuster, 1992).

Like most little girls, I longed for storybook castles while doubting my worth. The real tale of the People's Princess, as Diana was dubbed after her death, resonated with me. I wondered, more with each passing year, how many other precious women suffered inside the towers of their inner castles. Just as dedicated to performing a role in public. Just as isolated and miserable.

What would happen if someone told the truth? What if she lowered her mask, courageously, and showed her heart to those nearby?

As my Christ-esteem strengthened, a concern for my hidden sisters grew. So many others suffered in secret. Smiling at me from the crowds in the mall. Hurrying past me on the grocery aisles. Muttering self-curses in millions of cars lining the nation's roadways. I prayed, begging with clasped palms for someone to lift them up.

Yet, at the end of my prayers, I saw only my hands.

I thought I'd been transparent enough. I shared with a few clients— if it seemed relevant. But, I asked God, should I do more? Or is that *over*sharing?

Through years of prayer for the hurting, I realized God's answer often comes through us. If I wanted to *see* healing, I would need to lower my mask *first*.

I set aside my excuses and began to write, expecting the work to flow with ease.

Not so much.

Writing a personal book is *hard*, even after extensive growth and healing. Yet I knew I could not stop because the two motives within gave enough power to keep me going—His call and a hope my words might help someone.

The Lord called me to bear His image, to become the heroine of an entirely different war. He revealed the futility of battling divine allies, particularly myself. I had misdirected the strength God forged into my core. Christ encouraged me to stop fighting my namesake and redirect that innate ferocity against the real enemy. The sinister foe of all those whom God loves. I recognize him now for who he is: the captor who shackles women with lies and hides their names under false labels . . . like *unlovable.*

Inner healing takes courage and perseverance. Applying the principles in this book might challenge you. You will likely be tempted to doubt your strength. Please don't give up. Hold your hands in front of you, and remember your healing matters. To Christ and others. Someone else depends on you to get to the other side of the problem. From there, you can lift *them* up. Focus on your healer and those who need your mask to fall, then let the silent cries of other princesses grant you the courage to keep going.

Extreme Makeover God's Style: Identity Struggles in the Bible

Scripture Reference	Name	Who was mistaken about them?	How were they falsely identified?	How did God define them?
Genesis 17	Sarah	Sarah herself, and perhaps other women	Barren, too old to bear God's promise	Mother of nations
Genesis 37	Joseph	Brothers, Midianites	Brat worthy of death or slavery	Royal ruler who would rescue his people from famine
Genesis 39	Joseph	Potiphar and Potiphar's wife	Rapist, cheap fling	Innocent, noble
Exodus 3	Moses	Pharaoh, Hebrew people, and Moses himself	Murderer, lowly, poor speaker	God's representative, deliverer, a leader to his people

Scripture Reference	Name	Who was mistaken about them?	How were they falsely identified?	How did God define them?
Joshua 2	Rahab	Jericho	Insignificant, just a prostitute	Helper of God's people, great-grandmother to King David, ancestor of Christ
Judges 6	Gideon	Gideon himself, Israelites	Least significant member of the weakest family	Mighty warrior
1 Samuel 17	David	Goliath, David's brothers, King Saul	As powerless as a stick, pest	Victorious, next king of Israel, man after God's own heart
Matthew 1 Luke 1	Mary	Community	Defiled before marriage	Virgin mother of Christ
John 4	Samaritan Woman	Herself, community, lover	Harlot, outcast, not even worthy of betrothal	Evangelist to Samaria
John 9	Blind Man	Disciples	Sinful or of a sinful family	Ambassador of God's healing power
Luke 7	Woman who anoints Jesus with tears and perfume	Community	Harlot, sinful, undeserving of respectable company	Forgiven, anointer of Christ, worthy of mention in every retelling of the gospel
Throughout the New Testament	Jesus	Friends, family, hometown, religious leaders, political authorities, disciples	Heretic, liar, political activist, usurper of government, allied with evil	Lord, Son of God, Wonderful Counselor, Savior, Mighty King, Prince of Peace, Word Made Flesh

Empowerment Questions

1. Name a dream, passion, or calling. When have your self-doubts set obstacles in your life?

_____

_____

_____

_____

_____

2. What masks have you worn?

_____

_____

_____

_____

_____

3. Consider the extreme makeover list. Which biblical hero(es) do you relate to most, and why?

_____

_____

_____

_____

_____

4. Below, write all the slanderous names you've called yourself. Pray for the Lord to remove each one's scarred mark on your heart. At the top of the list, write, "In Christ, my name isn't."

_____

_____

_____

_____

_____

_____

5. Pray through Isaiah 49:16 and your favorite biblical hero's passage from our list. What do you hope to get from this book?

_____

_____

_____

_____

_____

_____

Chapter 2

FRONT LINES OF THE WAR WITHIN

Long before I became a counselor, as early as my childhood, other people's significance rang clear to me. My affirmations for others should have made it obvious that God's love *for me* made me just as valuable as everyone else. The explosions of "unlovable" dulled my inner ears for so long, I failed to hear the personal relevance in my words to others.

Yet, insecurity leverages its most ferocious attack upon our purpose. Encouragers become discouraged. Leaders tremble when standing at the threshold of growth. Artists struggle to feel motivated enough to continue to inspire others. Gifts and callings vary far beyond these few listed, but the sabotage remains the same.

While my writing and counseling suffered from dejection, your areas of insecurity may differ. But how can we recognize these vulnerable places? By considering our greatest strengths.

What potential do you possess to benefit others? Once you identify it (or them), that's most likely where fear will set its ambush.

Insecurity honors no terms of surrender. When you submit to fear, you lose more than a dream. Your gifts crash to the ground like weapons no longer available to defend the

Insecurity leverages its most ferocious attack upon our purpose.

helpless souls counting on your victory. Hope and joy drain from your heart as you assume the trudge of an enslaved war captive instead of fighting for a life of purpose. After years of enduring persistent attacks from this enemy, weariness tempts us to give up. Ease beguiles quitters into a slow, cruel death instead of their having chosen life.

Tracing War's Outbreak

My struggle with esteem can be traced as far back as first grade when I initially recognized myself as the "weird kid." I worked alone in classroom corners with Scholastic Reading Comprehension cards. Connecting with other kids my age seemed as futile as trying to embrace clouds. Friendships gathered in giggling circles so far from reach, I sometimes wondered if other people were real. By the time I reached junior high, I wondered if God was testing me. Maybe real life would begin after this sensory illusion. Not something a normal girl of ten contemplates, I know. Weird kid, remember?

Social isolation magnified my hunger for relationship. To a misfit like me, other hearts glowed with twenty-four-karat value. I was the refugee, gazing into Tiffany's ornate showroom from the bustling sidewalk hoping that if I brushed the dust from my coat shopkeepers would allow me to stand near the window and dream. I knew better than to step inside where others would notice my worthlessness. From outside, surrounded by people hurrying past, I could pretend.

As a teen, I observed well-liked, pretty girls. Like Colette, whose smile outshone her chestnut curls. Long lashes made her eyes look like stars. Even her clothes seemed to adore her. And even though she had a complexion smooth as cream, her genuine sweetness kept other girls from souring with jealousy. She was as beautiful "inside" as she was "out."

How can I be beautiful too? I wondered. Emulating her wouldn't work. I'd never pull off being a brunette, and I certainly couldn't afford a new wardrobe. And how silly would it look if I tried to act like her? There had to be a way to develop that *je ne sais quoi* defining beautiful people like her . . . some way to have a fragrant personality that drew others like the proverbial honeybee.

Oh, how delicious to be endearing from the inside out; if only others sought my company rather than simply tolerating my presence.

Academics worked both for and against me. While I was achieving personally, my high scores only seemed to blast huge craters to distance me from peers. This backfiring skill seemed my only asset, so I used it to conduct an informal survey. In order to win this battle against myself, I needed to define my goal, so I asked friends, acquaintances, and teachers the same question, "What does it mean to be beautiful?"

The results didn't support my intended outcome, however. Each person gave an entirely different answer. I concluded that a flaw in the question had invalidated the results.

It wasn't until later that I discovered the real error—I had aimed my question horizontally instead of vertically.

Despite believing in God, I anchored my identity outside of Him. I asked other people where to find esteem. They couldn't help me because my self-worth wasn't theirs to define. I had yet to learn that only the Creator can define purpose, and no human being can assess another's value. Nor her own. "Shall what is formed say to the one who formed it, 'Why did you make me like this?'" (Romans 9:20–21).

Anchoring my definition of beauty or likability in other people's opinions was like one sheep turning to another for shearing. Left unshorn, a sheep will perish no matter how many others bleat their sentiments toward them. Fellow sheep cannot remove the wool suffocating its life. Even the best members of a flock remain inept at the shepherd's role.

The greatest service "human sheep" can provide is to lead their friends to the Shepherd. Only the Shepherd can strip away the lies fleecing our identity and free us to live as our true selves.

Collateral Damage

Looting. Vandalism. Civilian casualties. Inner wars scathe more areas of our lives than we'd like to believe. More unfortunate still, our self-enmity wounds a vast population of bystanders.

I robbed myself by failing to acknowledge my glorious identity in Christ. Like many self-victimizers, I remained oblivious to my role and its impact on others. I would have stopped much sooner had I realized my slander toward God and its harmful effects on his children.

Self-definition affects *other* people. The Lord has called me to help his loved ones, but I can't offer them more than I believe I've got. If I perceive no assets, then I'll offer nothing beneficial to the world. Living with a false identity leaves my community without the unique blessings God created me to give.

Worse, the way I think of myself affects the way I treat people, which impacts how others think of themselves. This can inspire unhealthy behaviors in others. Self-deprecating attitudes can be contagious. Try watching someone else express fatigue with a yawn. How hard is it to resist yawning in response? Conversation works the same way. When someone puts herself down, others often follow suit.

For years, I failed to realize my low self-image affected more than me. I can only assume that the low-lying smoke on my battleground must have blinded me.

Biblical neon signs underscore the importance of debunking this myth of personality islands—as though one's character and nature doesn't affect anyone else. Not just some obscure Scripture, either; it's right there in the greatest commandments.

> Jesus replied: "'Love the Lord your God with all your heart and with all your soul and with all your mind.' This is the first and greatest commandment. And the second is like it: 'Love your neighbor as yourself.'"
>
> —Matthew 22:37–39

The greatest commandments are interconnected. We must love ourselves as sincerely as we love the Lord *and others*. Each component's strength affects the other two. How we love ourselves is related to our love for God and those God placed in our lives.

In the past, I've been my own worst enemy. I sent shrapnel flying in all directions. The damage I did exceeded vandalism or looting. I resisted my positive, God-crafted identity. Believing the unlovable lie crippled my ability to receive blessings or convey them. How much use could I be, then, if I remained outside the showroom windows, wishing I shared the twenty-four-karat significance of others?

Tactical Strategy: A Self-Love Framework

Self-enmity plagues the human experience. Too often we gaze with disgust at a distorted reflection of our identity. The struggle with our value takes place as deception fogs our view. We are now blind, and no battle can be won without the ability to see. Once able to see, we will stop fighting ourselves.

Truth clears away distorted beliefs so we can embrace our God-given identity. Generous amounts of Scripture will dissolve hateful thoughts and renew our vision. But this is not a one-time-only thing; it takes repeated polishing of our self-perception to attain a realistic gleam.

Esteem demands effort, yes, but we can never out-work God. He demonstrates time and again how much our significance matters. The Lord first established our worth when He took the time to create us. As though that weren't enough, He added love beyond all reason.

> For God so loved the world that he gave his one and only Son, that whoever believes in him shall not perish but have eternal life. For God did not send his Son into the world to condemn the world, but to save the world through him.
>
> —John 3:16–17

In 1 John, we see a connection between God's love for us, our sense of identity, and our ability to minister in Christ's name.

> See what great love the Father has lavished on us, that we should be called children of God! And that is what we are! The reason the world does not know us is that it did not know him. Dear friends, now we are children of God, and what we will be has not yet been made known. But we know that when he appears, we shall be like him, for we shall see him as he is. Everyone who has this hope in him purifies themselves, just as he is pure.
>
> —1 John 3:1–3

As divine *heirs*, our significance comes from our connection to the *Father* while security in our Christ-centered identity refreshes our soul. With these, odorous labels based on arrogance or self-abasement wash away.

> This is love: not that we loved God, but that he loved us and sent his Son as an atoning sacrifice for our sins.
>
> —1 John 4:10

Healthy esteem, or self-love, *begins with God's love for us.* We cannot extend His love to others effectively unless we accept it and abide in it ourselves.

First Corinthians 13 lists fourteen evaluators of love. As you read these, take a pen and your journal and write your answers to each aspect outlined. Redefine your self-perception to align with Christ's love using the verses as daily affirmations. Use your journal as part of discipleship conversations with your pastor or spiritual mentor. As you apply these principles to your self-relationship, observe the effects on the way you minister to others.

Patient
"Love is patient" (v. 4).
Are you patient with your own flaws, shortcomings, mistakes?

Kind
"Love is kind" (v. 4).
Is your self-talk kind? What are some of the things you do to care for yourself?

Free from jealousy
"It does not envy" (v. 4).
Do you feel free to rejoice with the freedoms, blessings, and happiness of others around you, even if you currently lack a comparable level of these things?

Not boastful or arrogant
"It does not boast, it is not proud" (v. 4).
Are you humble regarding your actions, talents, knowledge, and spirituality? Do you consider yourself equally valuable as others—all you have as a matter of grace?

Considerate, not rude
"It does not dishonor others" (v. 5).
Do you offer time and space for valuing your thoughts and feelings?
How do you honor yourself with the way you think, talk, and behave?

Unselfish
"It is not self-seeking" (v. 5).
Do you ask others how you can honor them and observe ways to
edify yourself and others in healthy balance? Who can you honor
this week, and how can you honor them?

Not easily angered
"It is not easily angered" (v. 5).
When circumstances become stressful, which thoughts or emotions do you give authority? How do you react to disappointment?
When you or others don't meet your expectations, what is your
emotional response? How many times in the past two weeks have
you lost your temper?

Forgiving, instead of record-keeping
"It keeps no record of wrongs" (v. 5).
Do you continue to think or talk about your mistakes for days,
weeks, or years afterward?

Does not delight in evil
"Love does not delight in evil" (v. 6).
Is gossip entertaining? Which of your behaviors do you feel the
need to justify, lest they seem like vices you should give up?

Honest
"Rejoices with the truth" (v. 6).
Do you, in prayer, ruthlessly seek honesty with yourself? Are you
willing to consider different points of view, even if the truth places

you at fault? Are you transparent before the Lord and those he places in close relationship with you? Name any areas in which you have been dishonest with yourself.

Protective

"It always protects" (v. 7).

Are you worth protecting? How uncomfortable is it to confront someone who is mistreating another person? Would you be willing to discourage someone from self-destructive behavior?

Trusting

"Always trusts" (v. 7).

We all know that not everyone is trustworthy. Are you trustworthy to yourself by sharing with others, yet maintaining ultimate responsibility for your emotional wellbeing? Can you trust God to be sufficient while relating to flawed beings?

Hopeful

"Always hopes" (v. 7).

Where is your hope? Hope that lasts is invested in eternal matters, not temporal conditions.

Persevering

"Always perseveres" (v. 7).

When do we throw in the towel on a ministry to which the Lord has clearly called us? When do we relinquish confidence in the identity God has bestowed upon us and give up on ourselves? Christ's love always perseveres. Salvation wraps our lives in his enduring devotion. We dwell in Him, where His strength offers ongoing renewal. With the "always" love of our Savior, we never need to give up.

Empowerment Questions

1. How do you have the potential to benefit others? Try to name your strength(s), issues that prick your heart (homelessness, for example), or spiritual gifts.

_____

_____

_____

_____

2. Have you experienced discouragement or setbacks in these areas? If so, how?

_____

_____

_____

_____

3. Draw a timeline and note emotionally charged experiences from childhood to the present. How did you feel about others and yourself at different ages? How might your perspective during those painful times compare to that of a loving God?

_____

_____

_____

_____

4. Can you identify key moments in your past that triggered self-doubt? Pray the scriptural truth of your identity as a child of God over these memories.

_____

_____

_____

_____

_____

_____

5. Prayerfully consider the self-love strategy. Name the specific area(s) for which you'll ask the Holy Spirit to help you grow and heal.

_____

_____

_____

_____

_____

_____

Chapter 3

A FRENEMY'S LIES

M*ost Likely to Succeed.* Decades have passed since the yearbook staff printed those words under my photo. At the time, I thought the title confirmed my plan to earn significance, since obviously no one would love me for my personality.

Many years later I stared into the mirror at my sunken-eyed reflection. Dull, mousy hair frayed from its clip and frizzed at splitting ends. I leaned in to get a closer view of my skin's gray tones. My pupils expanded to eclipse my blue irises with darkness.

I glanced at the prediction of my future again, reading each word slowly: Most. Likely. To. Succeed.

But I had not lived up to anyone's expectation of success. Not theirs. Not mine.

I was a failure.

Accusations tumbled at my helpless image in the mirror.

Failure to earn a self-supportive living. Internally, I listed the attempts in various careers that never amounted to a respectable salary.

Failure to be the perfect mom. While my kids seemed to do well, it was probably in spite of my mothering abilities not because of them.

I loved them, but had I done enough for them? Would I ever know the total number of mistakes I'd made while rearing them?

Failure to be loved. Perhaps, I pondered, my husband would be happier with someone more energetic, more fun, and just . . . well, more.

Failure to do great things for God. I narrowed my eyes at the wretch before me. Skills, education, supportive family—spoilage of resources. So much had been given to me, and what did I have to show for it? Nothing. I earned no return on blessings.

Surely even God was disappointed in me.

The sorry reflection blurred as I twisted the lie's blade to deepen the wound. Others deserved to take the opportunities I had squandered. I once heard God would reallocate a resistant person's ministry. I couldn't blame Jesus if He did that with mine.

But this lie was the cruelest of all, so I attacked with this weapon more often than any other. Nothing could shelter me from the barrage of hate. I couldn't retreat or flee to escape battle. Brutalized by my thoughts, nowhere remained safe. I was the ultimate insider, conspiring to exploit my weaknesses. When I should have treated myself like a best friend, I delivered betrayal instead. I'd become my own nemesis. A frenemy, so to speak.

I'm not alone in my traitorous crimes. But in the midst of battle, I felt that way. The din of attacks dulled my awareness of commonality. I attempted to reach others with compassion, but shelling resounded in my ears to dismiss the whisper. That peaceful voice suggesting transparency might help someone else, but no . . .

The frenemy ramped up her assault. I could not expose my contemptible soul. I kept my scars buried deep within the twisted rebar and mounds of rubble.

Inability to trust yourself makes life tougher than necessary.

I didn't recognize the significance of my critical attitude. In frenemy-speak, I justified the abuse as a long, hard look at myself or as some form of humility. Motivation. Discipline. Then my nemesis leaned in closer for the stab. I sabotaged my hope and stole life's blessings. Ironic, how I didn't see my own attack strategy. But that's probably because the plan for my destruction didn't originate with me.

A greater, more insidious enemy suggested each and every lie. I failed to realize my behavior ran deeper than self-harm. When I derided myself and sabotaged God's purpose for me and through me, I acted in compliance with Satan.

Had I realized my treachery pitted me against God, I would have ended the war much sooner.

Failure—the "f" word that no longer applies to those redeemed by Christ—is only one of the countless lie-weapons waged against us in our minds.

> *When I derided myself and sabotaged God's purpose for me and through me, I acted in compliance with Satan.*

Stupid. Worthless. Ugly. Awkward. Good-for-nothing. Only-good-for-one-thing.

The messages adapt and grow. Experiences can plant them, as when slander echoes from the past until we believe and adopt it. Or we can develop inferences about our lives, and the lies seem to form in our minds on their own. Whether the words begin in others' lips or our own minds, the enemy of our souls facilitates the attack. We choose if we will let his propaganda jingles continue to play in our heads.

Not all frenemy lies begin with a negative slant, but they usually end there. Sometimes the enemy deceives us with pride.

You could run the company better than the corporate gorilla. You're the only smart driver. You deserve some indulgence.

With the exception of narcissists and sociopaths, the tumble from pride to shame tends to be predictable. The enemy attacks with a pride lie, then hits you with a shame lie on the back side after the ego-party fizzles out.

The enemy chooses the personal words for each destructive campaign but uses similar techniques to trap us with them. Just like an advertising plan, there's a strategy. He applies a similar tactical pattern to get us to buy into any junk he wants to use against us.

To understand what makes these lies so effective, we must first dissect the elements of a successful lie:

1. Truth

The most effective lie starts with a little bit of truth. Not enough to make it true, but enough to make it powerful. For example, Satan reminded me of my low income—factual information. Equating small earnings with failure warped the message and rendered it untrue. But its opening fact had snared my attention.

2. Emotional Charge

Great lies add an inappropriate emotional slant to the facts. Embellishment or exaggeration enhances the power of a negative charge. For example, take the lies aimed at creating parental insecurity. This evil strategy capitalizes upon love for children to burrow deep into a sore spot. By design. *I should've protected my children from all harm. Have I caused irreparable damage? What if they refuse to seek counseling because I'm a therapist? Their misery will pass on to their children because I failed. Our entire family line is doomed.* Emotional energy distracts us from glaring truths and draws us into a negative, escalating thought pattern. Shame tempts parents to ignore the fact that perfection only exists in Jesus Christ and not us as parents. We can "should" ourselves to death, but shame fails to alter past mistakes or render us blameless today. Anxiety, with its penchant for exaggeration, often slinks in as shame's villainous bestie while worry blinds us from recognizing God's sufficiency to handle what parents cannot.

3. Illusion

There are several ways a lie can mesmerize us into accepting it. Similar to a magician's technique, lies can distract our attention to focus on something that seems relevant but remains far from the real action. Equating or relating the irrelevant remains a common technique. Satan whispers comparisons into our thoughts, and we don't recognize he's comparing apples to bread. An effective way to mislead someone is to create a train of logic that sounds logical *but isn't really true.*

Circular reasoning exemplifies this verbal sleight of hand. In the movie *God's Not Dead*, a pivotal moment in the debate over the validity of faith hinges upon the following quote from Stephen Hawking in his book *The Grand Design*: "Because there is a law such as gravity, the universe can and will create itself from nothing. It is not necessary to invoke God to light the blue touch paper and set the Universe going."

The professor in the film cites this quote as an irrefutable argument against the existence of God. Though unable to comprise a rebuttal at first, Josh Wheaton (a Christian student) soon realizes this is a circular argument, which attempts to prove itself without any valid external points. Any circular argument sounds logical if examined without further information. If we didn't have additional information about the effects of dehydration, we could be led to believe the body's existing water content proves our biological ability to self-hydrate without obtaining water.

In addition to circular reasoning, the enemy twists God's words to distort their meaning. For me, "success equals income" does not line up with the Bible's overall message. Neither does earning God's approval by some kind of return-on-investment logic. Pulled out of context, Luke 19:12–26 seems to indicate the Lord loves productive servants most.

> A man of noble birth . . . called ten of his servants and gave them
> ten minas. . . . Then he sent for the servants to whom he had given
> the money, in order to find out what they had gained with it. . . .
> He replied, "I tell you that to everyone who has, more will be given,
> but as for the one who has nothing, even what they have will be
> taken away."

At first glance, we could presume God favors those who do the most with their gifts. When read along with the whole of Scripture, God's consistent heart-focus shines through and reveals the main issue of this passage as an emphasis on the servants' attitudes toward their master. How many years did the widow Anna (Luke 2) wait in the Temple before offering her single recorded prophecy? Attitude matters more than the quantity of good deeds performed. And our spiritual disposition toward God is precisely the area our enemy intends to derail.

Frenemy lies remain a common struggle because they're as ancient and ingrained into our nature as sin. Literally. Our first lies came from the enemy warping God's words in Eden. And Eve partnered with him.

> He said to the woman, "Did God really say, 'You must not eat from
> any tree in the garden'?" The woman said to the serpent, "We may
> eat fruit from the trees in the garden, but God did say, 'You must
> not eat fruit from the tree that is in the middle of the garden, and
> you must not touch it, or you will die.'"
>
> —Genesis 3:1–3

Compare this to God's actual command to Adam in Genesis 2:17: "You must not eat from the tree of the knowledge of good and evil, for when you eat from it you will certainly die." Satan adjusted the words to "any tree." Eve instituted the first example of legalism by adding, "and you must not touch it." Satan started with truth, preyed upon the emotional fears of restrictive authority figures, and distracted humanity from his actual agenda of distancing them from their trusting relationship with God.

The enemy snared them with pride lies first, saying, "When you eat from it your eyes will be opened, and you will be like God" (Genesis 3:5). Shame hit immediately after sin. "The eyes of both of them were opened, and they realized they were naked . . . and they hid from the LORD God" (vv. 7–8). Satan had caught them again.

In Matthew 4:1–11, Satan used the same tactics against Jesus. He dangled food to tempt Jesus' senses then went on to tempt Him with power as he twisted God's words to use against Him.

But *because Christ resisted the lies and put sin to death on the Cross,* we no longer remain helpless to their enchantments. He invites us to participate in an effective defense strategy.

But we first need to identify Satan as the enemy and stop fighting against ourselves. Though prideful, the devil prefers to remain off our radar. His best attacks remain those he can use to pin the blame on us and keep the focus off of the true culprit. As the Great and Powerful Oz put it in the film *The Wizard of Oz*, "Pay no attention to that man behind the curtain."

We first need to identify Satan as the enemy and stop fighting against ourselves.

Once we pull back the veil we can deal with the deceiver. Acknowledging a toxic pattern is the first step toward removing barriers to a victorious life of purpose and blessings. I couldn't begin overcoming self-enmity until I recognized my battle and identified attack points of entry.

How did I recognize an unseen war? As mold rots a home, its spores permeate the air until they poison the lungs of people who dwell there. Likewise, insidious spiritual forces often leave destructive traces in plain view.

Shame infested my body and soul, crawling under my skin like a parasite. I tried extreme diets, exercise, extra layers of makeup. My emotions declined. I couldn't work myself out of the pit. Social activities failed to cheer me. Isolation besieged me, even in crowds. Nothing eased my discomfort with the sight of myself. My face darkened in the mirror, scowling at every inner and outer insufficiency. My relationships grew distant and ineffective, despite my attempts to fake a sense of connection. The war wounds got worse and proved untreatable at the surface. These stubborn, visible signs alerted me that underlying problem existed.

An enemy had burrowed deep into my soul and was eating me alive from the inside out. Pestilent lies invaded, encamped within, and turned my own mind against me. Holes in my life had allowed the nemesis easy access. I examined my problems to find his patterns and traced them to misleading thoughts and toxic attitudes.

Several clues help us recognize misleading thoughts. The primary red flag for fraudulent thinking is a shift away from God-centeredness. Comparison, self-reliance, or doubting the goodness of God should trigger alarms of an enemy attack. Comparison to others or secular standards distracts us from honoring God's purpose. This happens with prideful and shameful perspectives. Arrogant piety creates the illusion of peering down on less holy neighbors. Those who climb onto a self-idolatry pedestal doom themselves to fall. Insecurity over circumstances or performance creates a blindness to Christ's sovereignty.

Sometimes we try to take matters into our own hands without seeking help from God. We think we can cover certain things without His guidance. When disrespected, for example, we might react in self-justified fury without seeking divine insight. Why bother praying about which job to take when we should obviously choose the most lucrative? We've always driven, eaten, worshipped, [fill in the blank] this way, so there's no need to consult Jesus.

While we don't consider involving God in details, He longs to fill our entire lives. Most of the life we live is in the details we consider too insignificant for God.

A sinister foe wages both overt battle and stealthy attacks, plotting to use our minds to betray us. We need more than back-up or a bigger weapon than self-reliance. And we have a far greater, more powerful ally to take down his lies. Truth Incarnate loves us beyond our imagination, dying to save us from darkness. We need to arm ourselves against the lies by covering our minds, hearts, and souls with His presence. When we immerse ourselves in Scripture and prayer, dressing our spirits in the armor of God, Christ offers more than assistance or back-up. He fights the battle and strengthens us to stand.

> Put on the full armor of God, so that you can take your stand against the devil's schemes. For our struggle is not against flesh and blood, but against the rulers, against the authorities, against the powers of this dark world and against the spiritual forces of evil in the heavenly realms. Therefore put on the full armor of God, so that when the day of evil comes, you may be able to stand your ground, and after you have done everything, to stand. Stand firm then, with the belt of truth buckled around your waist, with the breastplate of righteousness in place, and with your feet fitted with the readiness that comes from the gospel of peace. In addition to

all this, take up the shield of faith, with which you can extinguish all the flaming arrows of the evil one. Take the helmet of salvation and the sword of the Spirit, which is the word of God. And pray in the Spirit on all occasions with all kinds of prayers and requests.

—Ephesians 6:11–18

Tactical Strategy: Lie Disarmament

Self-criticism can be directed inward and ricochet onto others. Both kinds of destruction can be alleviated by targeting the source. A strategy known as cognitive monitoring helps identify negative self-talk.

Cognitive monitoring refers to paying attention to how you think. Keeping track of thoughts and beliefs helps us discover any unhealthy patterns. Then we must exchange the toxic messages for life-giving truths.

In order to identify existing internal lies ask yourself two questions: What messages play inside your mind when you make a mistake? What messages play inside your mind when others don't respond positively to you?

Think about whether you talk to yourself politely and respectfully. Do you speak to others in the same manner? Vandalizing self-definitions might include:

I am . . .
not valuable.
a failure.
unlovable.
incompetent.
guilty.
useless.

supposed to have control over my life.

not allowed to feel or show certain emotions.

ill-equipped to minister to others.

unable to change.

Test negative thoughts for the following distortion clues:

Your thoughts don't correlate with scriptural definitions of those beloved by God.

The statement involves hyperbole or absolutes, such as "always" or "never."

A broken record of shame statements becomes your theme music for memories, indicating you have not accepted forgiveness and grace.

The message includes "should" statements about the past or present, instead of action steps for improving your life.

We cannot end the process by removing negative self-messages because we do not function with thought vacuums. Instead, we must replace lies with scriptural truths, using positive quotes or favorite verses to craft healthy patterns of inner thoughts. Employ the Scripture lists included in this book, then add favorites of your own. Write out and post your affirmations where you'll see them often. Renew the posted statements weekly so the words retain fresh impact.

Secure that belt of truth, sister. You're suiting up as a mighty warrior. It might take time to get accustomed to your destined duds, but rest assured—this Christ-confidence does you justice.

Empowerment Questions

1. Do your thoughts often include slander about yourself? List your frenemy lies.

   _____

   _____

   _____

   _____

   _____

2. How might your self-doubts be limiting potential blessings in your life?

   _____

   _____

   _____

   _____

3. Which relationships have an opportunity to improve as you develop Christ-centered self-esteem?

   _____

   _____

   _____

   _____

4. Consider the lie disarmament strategy. Use a scrap of paper or an app to track your thoughts throughout the week. Replace each vandalizing self-statement with an affirmation of your position as a daughter of the Most High. What lies have you battled this week?

_____

_____

_____

_____

_____

_____

5. Who else could benefit from these affirmations? List their names, and share your newfound words of esteem.

_____

_____

_____

_____

_____

_____

Chapter 4

THE COMPARISON TRAP

At nineteen, I cowered behind other girls at the Islamorada dock. They cooed at the muscled guy perched on his speedboat. *Let them drool over him*, I thought. With their perfect tans and beach-perfect bodies, they belonged out front where they could be seen.

But not me.

Even though my hip bones poked out further than my stomach, I didn't feel thin enough. I was too pale to wear a swimsuit. And doesn't white make everything appear larger?

What am I doing here, anyway?

I only wanted to hide.

Even today, memories of that experience trigger a temptation to question my appearance all over again. My hip bones no longer poke out, and thinner girls grin at me from every magazine ad and television show. The world's beauty standards snarl into my psyche: *put down that bag of chips and run to the gym.*

But I won't. If I give those snarky thoughts a toehold, negativity will consume my mind. The attack on my esteem can derail my purpose. Dwelling on comparison to others distracts me from serving God's will for others. I must laser my focus.

The Master Artist created me to deliver more value than low weight or a tan. Because I'm alive, God ordained important work for me to focus on. But to start, I must accept *myself*. If I don't, I cannot bring a blessing to *others*.

It takes awareness and strategy to avoid the enemy's pitfalls. Even after progress in healing, temptations attack. At times, the comparison trap continues to yawn its serrated jaws on my path via fashion trends not designed for my body type and successful twentysomething, slender women. Sometimes I step on the trigger and comparison's jaws clamp into my flesh. Other times, I saunter past it with a smile. It just depends upon how I'm walking at that place on the path.

My vulnerability to this and other traps depends upon how well prepared I am to recognize and avert the pitfall. Certain conditions weaken my awareness. Untended stress. Inadequate prayer time. Unresolved anger or bitterness. Isolation from healthy Christian fellowship. Lack of rest. Letting the guardian of my thought patterns go to sleep on the job.

The Lord can help me manage stress . . . if I submit it to Him. And He can sustain me through brief periods of inadequate sleep. But the problem comes when I take a general lifestyle shift away from spiritual healthiness and toward complacency. It's less effort to allow things to slide in a negative direction. To shorten meditation time. To miss a few activities every week with church friends.

It's easier to ignore my patterns.

The enemy's lifestyle choices are effortless but complicated and murky. God's lifestyle choices are simple and clear but not so easy.

Comparing ourselves to others comes naturally. We size ourselves up to the standards staring at us. Living out the comparison lifestyle involves a complicated list of futile tasks and emotional crises. We can't win an endless race against others. To remain prettier, more successful, and better liked than everyone around us flickers out of reach. We exhaust ourselves chasing the mirage of an impossible goal. In the midst of striving to measure up, we lose our God-given identity.

I wasn't created to be tan. Or thinner than my friends. Or the richest CEO on the planet. Or the most successful Christian author. Or the highest-paid, most sought-after therapist. God created me to honor and obey him as *Tina*. To lay myself down as well as my plans and the gifts He crafted into my soul. No matter who I size myself up to, it'll always be an "apples to whales" comparison. I'll never speak like Beth Moore, write like Max Lucado, or look like Cindy Crawford. And that's not just a *good* thing. It's a *God* thing.

Because we were never meant to be the same.

God's no-comparison plan is simple: don't compare yourself to other people.

Elementary to comprehend, right? A bit more difficult to maintain. It takes intentional realignment to stay on track. Our human nature continually pulls us off the best path for our lives. We stray off into the high grass beyond the path's edge, where the enemy loves to hide his traps. But there are a few defensive techniques to help protect our minds from veering into risky areas.

Defense #1: Thought Monitoring

The brain defaults to "routine" as a time- and energy-saving feature. We react to people and events according to a pattern. When neighbors wave, they're demonstrating friendship . . . or showing off their new car . . . or pointing out the immaculate lawn they're trimming.

How we interpret a situation depends on our attitudes. An attitude reflects a pattern of thoughts we've accepted.

Our minds respond to circumstances according to how we program our thoughts. We either allow subconscious processes to develop the pattern or take an intentional role in guiding it. Left unguarded, our minds roll downhill with comparisons and other unhealthy attitudes. Ruts known as neural pathways form after years of these default responses. And if we allow negative patterns to continue, they will.

In high school, I debated the predictability of human nature with our school psychologist. He maintained people do not change. A person walks through a doorway the same way every time. He argued this hopeless, creature-of-habit concept with fervor. For an hour. Yet despite his use of jargon, I continued to disagree with his perspective.

I still believe the defining mark of humanness is our capacity to change.

I don't remember if I did it to prove my point, but I changed my handwriting in high school. Before it became my current style, I had to choose what to practice. I loved the typewriter-styled "a" in my English teacher's print and the flourish classic authors added to their capital letters. I planned and practiced a new pattern.

Now it is my default response.

Rather than allowing my mind to accept a default response of comparison, I choose healthy thoughts to put in place. When old triggers tempt me to compare myself to thinner girls, I can recall esteeming truths instead. I remind myself to shift my thoughts back where they belong. I have preset messages to underscore the spiritual worth of the other person and myself.

God didn't create me according to earthly standards. He didn't set another person as a model to copy when crafting my features. The Ultimate Artist simultaneously sculpted me in His image and designed me as an original work. Why should I measure my characteristics against another person as the perfect model? If I should aspire to become more like *any* model, it ought to be him.

However, you cannot extinguish unhealthy attitudes until you've identified them. To pinpoint downhill trends, pay attention to your thought patterns. Increase your awareness of comparison temptations. Jot down a quick symbol or phrase in a notepad (a phone app works fine too) each time your mind veers into comparison. Write out your results in a journal at the end of each day. Over time, journaling reveals the frequency and triggers of negative thoughts. If you know when you're most vulnerable to comparisons, you can adjust to improve your chance at success.

Defense #2: Environmental Filtering

Create an environment for healthy attitudes by limiting exposure to triggers. When counseling girls who struggled with body image, I recommended avoiding fashion magazines. Beauty pageants aren't the only events promoting the judgment of women by physical standards. An abundance of television shows and films emphasize their heroines' zero-sized frame. Most video and print media airbrush a subject's features. (In 2002, actress Jamie Lee Curtis posed for *More* magazine with the intent that her photos would be unretouched because she wanted young girls to see that she wasn't perfect and had plenty of flaws. The results of her decision were profound and effectual.[6])

Those sensitive to appearance comparisons *must* screen their viewing habits.

Some find others' progress motivating, but some shrivel when the neighboring gym machine displays twice their pace. When issues center on performance, competitive activities can trigger insecurity or encourage an ongoing need for affirmation. To combat this, try puzzles

---

6. Bobbi Brown, "Our Beauty Hero: An Unretouched Jamie Lee Curtis," Yahoo!, March 8, 2015, https://www.yahoo.com/beauty/our-beauty-hero-an-unretouched-jamie-lee-curtis -113020098248.html.

or all-win games for a while. As you add back low-intensity contests in small doses, refuse to entertain comparison mindsets. Instead, redefine the purpose as an opportunity to share quality time with friends or family. Practice celebrating each chance to support loved ones, and in this way you win every time.

Cut back on measurement collection. Stay off the scale. Do your best without a constant eye on the quota charts. Don't ask how others are doing in order to compare results.

Although you can't eliminate every opportunity for comparison, you can filter out some of the toxic prompts—certain magazines, media, and social circles promote a comparison mentality. If you can't toss these out of your life completely, reduce the amount of time spent with them.

Defense #3: Fellowship

After clearing the negative influences from your environment, add the positives. Quickly. Thought patterns will revert or find another detrimental rut if not replaced. Immerse yourself in the company of uplifting people who resist entertaining comparisons. When you find a supportive circle, enlist a couple of trustworthy friends to help keep you accountable on the journey to healthier thinking.

Defense #4: Scripture

Take a moment to look over the creation story in Genesis chapters 1 and 2. Now, notice the word *oops* is absent. God did not say of anything He made, "Boy, I really messed that up, didn't I?" Five times in the first chapter of Genesis, the Lord evaluated His creative work "and saw that it was good." This includes a positive assessment of the way He made human beings.

Then we read, "Adam and his wife were both naked, and they felt no shame" (Genesis 2:25). Women tend to have higher body fat content than men, but Eve didn't look down at the extra padding around her middle and say, "I can't *wait* until someone invents liposuction." Nor did Adam wonder whether Eve would be more impressed with bigger muscles. Despite many attempts by artists to depict physical perfection in the original couple, Genesis contains no details regarding their appearance. There are no specifics about the size of feet, ears, or noses. We don't know the color of their skin, eyes, or hair. None of the measures by which we judge beauty were relevant in Eden. God made it and declared it good. End of evaluation.

Creating a healthier thought pattern starts with choosing positive messages. Craft a list of affirmations to help resist each comparison temptation. Scripture serves as a helpful resource to trounce self-defeating thoughts. With affirmations, reminders, and verses, plan the new style of thinking. Writing out the list provides an additional way for your mind to absorb the positive thoughts scrolled across the lines. It also offers a visual reminder to keep you on track.

Defense #5: Prayer

The most powerful tool for renewing your mind is the Creator himself. Lean on your best resource through frequent prayer. Ask the Holy Spirit to search your thoughts through daily meditation. Take a few minutes to confess your recent thought struggles and request God's transforming presence. Then, listen. Allow yourself to soak in Christ's grace and truth. Even if you don't hear a specific message, enjoy a time of believing God's love as the nullifying factor regarding comparison.

In addition to deeper sessions, shoot brief prayers for help as needed throughout the day. Allow the Holy Spirit to help you catch negative thoughts. When temptations flare up, turn to prayer as your *first* resort rather than the *next* or *last* one. Together with your list of truths, you'll stand against temptation with incomparable protection.

Defense #6: Create a No-Comparison Zone

We adopt the reality we create about ourselves. If we allow comparison myths to govern our standards of self-worth, our true destiny will remain obscure. We can never be someone else, nor should we try to be. Attempting to measure up to others keeps us from becoming who *we* are meant to become. Wasting effort on an impossible goal of comparing to another person prohibits us from actualizing the unique potential with which God created us.

Draw or copy this reminder symbol. Post it where you find yourself most prone to falling into comparison traps.

In addition, keep the following Scripture passages in mind to deflect temptations for comparison:

> For you created my inmost being; you knit me together in my mother's womb. I praise you because I am fearfully and wonderfully made; your works are wonderful, I know that full well.
>
> — Psalm 139:13–14

A heart at peace gives life to the body, but envy rots the bones.

—Proverbs 14:30

You will keep in perfect peace those whose minds are steadfast, because they trust in you.

—Isaiah 26:3

"Teacher, which is the greatest commandment in the Law?" Jesus replied: "'Love the Lord your God with all your heart and with all your soul and with all your mind.' . . . And the second is like it: 'Love your neighbor as yourself.'"

—Matthew 22:36–39

Do not conform to the pattern of this world, but be transformed by the renewing of your mind. Then you will be able to test and approve what God's will is—his good, pleasing and perfect will.

—Romans 12:2

Love is patient, love is kind. It does not envy.

—1 Corinthians 13:4

Since we live by the Spirit, let us keep in step with the Spirit. Let us not become conceited, provoking and envying each other.

—Galatians 5:25–26

You were taught, with regard to your former way of life, to put off your old self, which is being corrupted by its deceitful desires; to be made new in the attitude of your minds; and to put on the new self, created to be like God in true righteousness and holiness.

—Ephesians 4:22–24

Submit yourselves, then, to God. Resist the devil, and he will flee from you. Come near to God and he will come near to you. Wash your hands, you sinners, and purify your hearts, you double-minded.

—James 4:7–8

Humble yourselves before the Lord, and he will lift you up.

—James 4:10

Therefore, rid yourselves of all malice and all deceit, hypocrisy, envy, and slander of every kind.

—1 Peter 2:1

Be alert and of sober mind. Your enemy the devil prowls around like a roaring lion looking for someone to devour. Resist him, standing firm in the faith, because you know that the family of believers throughout the world is undergoing the same kind of sufferings.

—1 Peter 5:8–9

For the word of God is alive and active. Sharper than any double-edged sword, it penetrates even to dividing soul and spirit, joints and marrow; it judges the thoughts and attitudes of the heart.

—Hebrews 4:12

Empowerment Questions

1. What negative beliefs might you need to change?

_____

_____

_____

_____

_____

2. Have you compared yourself to others? If so, whom?

_____

_____

_____

_____

_____

3. Which environmental triggers might you need to avoid?

_____

_____

_____

_____

_____

4. Do you have encouraging fellowship? If so, how often? How can you enhance your sister-strengthening opportunities (e.g. join a small group or Bible study)?

_____

_____

_____

_____

_____

_____

5. Print or draw the no-comparison zone graphic. Which Scripture will you post with it first?

_____

_____

_____

_____

_____

_____

Chapter 5

THE MYTH OF HUMAN APPROVAL

As a college freshman, I buckled under the pressure of my friend's plea to go onto the stage with her. She dragged me by the arm, insistent. Begging. Maggie even employed the irresistible deal closer: her pouty-faced guilt trip.

Soon enough, she peered over my shoulder as I scrawled my signature on the waiver.

A deejay interviewed us at the foot of the steps leading to the stage. I struggled to mutter a response. His voice faded behind the blaring horror facing me—a bikini contest.

Acid churned in my gut. Why had I let Maggie talk me into such a nightmare? I scanned the lakeside park surrounding the stage, desperate for a coat (or tree trunk or something) to hide my mayonnaise-pale skin. My chin sank, which called my attention to a fist-sized bruise on my left thigh. Extra ugliness to parade out there.

Super.

The crowd's buzzing grew and pressed closer to the stage. Laughter and shouts swelled in the student throng of two hundred. Or was it three hundred? I couldn't tell and didn't want to know. The voices quelled to a murmur as the deejay announced the first contestant's name.

An assistant tapped the sun-bronzed arm of the first girl in line. She flipped a pale lock of hair, which seemed to glow against her coppery shoulder. The curvy blonde strutted to the center of the platform. The crowd rallied as she wriggled her shoulders forward and back, as if testing whether her swimsuit's lime-green triangles might burst off.

Forget it; I was not *about* to do that. I hugged my knobby elbows, hoping to fold into myself and disappear. But the handler found me.

"You're next."

The temporary stairs had no railing. I wavered as I trudged up five enormous steps. The platform swam before me. I stared at the black surface. Terrified, I shuffled toward center stage. Fervent noise churned before me. Though unable to discern jeers from applause, I felt the crowd's body evaluations pelting my pale, bruised flesh on display before them.

I couldn't have hustled across the stage faster if I'd been chased with a flame thrower. After stumbling down the exit stairs, the blood pounding in my ears finally eclipsed the brutal chants.

Maggie beamed as she rushed up to me and grabbed both my arms. I don't recall my exact words, but I might have threatened to kill her if she didn't get far away from me . . . and right then.

No matter what anyone said, or how much they pleaded, I determined never again to subject myself to such a barbaric experience.

If only I'd protected myself as well as I planned.

Although I never entered another bikini or beauty-related contest, subjecting myself to others' judgment recurred with devastating frequency. And just like the college venue, I volunteered for it. Sometimes, I even shirked wisdom for a chance at the world's most addictive substance—human approval.

I sought acceptance as if it breathed life into my bones. While some approval-seekers home in on a specific area, I pursued them all. I thirsted for compliments regarding my appearance, performance, and personality. Accolades dosed me like tablespoons of syrup. Their sweet flavor faded into doubtful aftertastes, leaving me thirstier than ever.

Approval dependency crept in without warning. It seemed normal to want people to like me. In fact, my desires harmonized with those swirling in conversations around me. Everyone else appeared to share my craving. And the sense of normalcy goaded my yearning for acceptance.

Approval addiction begins in childhood. We dope up on remarks about our new outfits, stickers on our papers, and getting asked to come over to play. Though none are evil on their own, a growing covetousness for them proves devastating. Fragile to begin with, self-esteem lands in critical condition when it depends upon other people's reactions.

As unwitting conspirators in our demise, we sign ourselves up for outward and internal forms of judgment. Approval seeking occurs in three basic areas: appearance, performance, and personality. We can seek acceptance in one area or go all-out, like I did. I bring good news for all those across the spectrum. Freedom is possible regardless of the issue's pervasiveness.

Appearance Approval

Despite wide admiration, celebrities often develop deep insecurities about their appearance. Katie Couric, Thandie Newton, and Paula Abdul represent dozens of stars who report having suffered from eating disorders. One of the most famous examples, Karen Carpenter, died at age thirty-two from complications related to anorexia.

Body image issues aren't reserved for the famous. Their struggles reflect a rampant social pattern of insecurity about appearance. A 2015 study by Common Sense Media revealed more than half of girls and about a third of boys between ages six and eight report believing they should be thinner.[7]

Insecurity about appearance surfaces in more ways than eating disorders. From countercultural teens to rising businesspeople, all subsets of society send a clear message: the dress must impress. Whether it's an everyday struggle or limited to certain occasions, perhaps you've shared my wardrobe-wresting experience: Does this *fit*? Not too casual but not pretentious. Calming colors or inspiring?

I've been late more than once fighting with these simple decisions.

And clothing isn't the only way appearance approval takes hold of our mindset. A wisp of graying hair glowers at us in the mirror. Ms. Neat Freak knocks at the door for an unannounced visit and finds the beds unmade, toys scattered, and a pile of laundry near the front door. A person who once embraced us with compliments now hurries off with little or no praise.

Fear whistles in through the cracks of our esteem. What will people think? And on that chilling draft comes the whisper of vanity and all her favorite lies.

Concern about what others think can crop up like a harmless-looking weed in the most unlikely places—ministry included. "Don't tell *anyone* you made a mistake," we tell ourselves. "Hide the flaws. Perfect your game-face. No tears and no errant confessions." We don't allow ourselves opportunities for true protection, growth, or healing. Despair and ineffective relationships mark only the start of a long list of emotional consequences.

When Christian leaders worry more about what people think than what God thinks, the results can also create havoc in their communities and families. The world approves of those who spritz themselves with its

---

7. Common Sense Media. "Children, Teens, Media, and Body Image: A Common Sense Media Research Brief." San Francisco, CA: Common Sense Media, 2015. Available at https://www .commonsensemedia.org/research/children-teens-media-and-body-image.

familiar sin-scents. A little error here and there proves acceptable. Not intending to trespass as far as those other serious offenders, of course. Until the people-pleasing temptations lead them further than intended. Flirtations become affairs. Self-centeredness turns into abuse of power. Indulgence takes root as an addiction. A little trespass, left unchecked, can hijack a faith community or family into devastation lasting for years.

We can try to wrap infinite layers of "normal" lies over our souls, but the cover hampers our ministry instead of helping it along. When we hide to gain the approval of our peers, we inhibit the healing God intends to use in our ministry to others. The condition of our heart affects each rippling echo of its beat. Appearance approval undermines the positive impact of our lives and can prove toxic to our souls.

Jesus never campaigned for a kingdom of whitewashed surfaces. He poured out his life for the grit-to-grace truth. Yet in our compulsion to appear perfect, we find ourselves working against our Savior. Turning our focus from God's will deprives our vision of clarity.

Performance Approval

After countless rejections and a slew of financial losses, giving up on writing not only seemed easy but logical. People had even made fun of me. The streak of failures and critical echoes blared to muffle encouragement. Why should I pursue a goal that made no sense?

Yet one thing held my chin above the waves of despair. Not editorial praise, which faded after a few months' glow. Nor the pile of awards gracing the top of my filing cabinet, which the publishing world forgot in a matter of weeks.

My purpose survived on invisible words.

Amid the din of rejections and praises, the Lord's whisper resounded in my spirit. "I have called you to write."

God never asked me to win the world's approval. He didn't commission me to impress everyone or exact spotless performance. My fulfillment rested instead upon obeying with all my heart.

Thirst for acceptance goes beyond surface issues. Vanity isn't skin deep. Rather it burrows its claws into the muscle of our purpose. We pine for approval, not just of our outer layers but of all we do.

The arena of praise-seeking differs from one individual to the next, but the underlying nature remains constant. A mother winces at criticism of her child's behavior. Employees scour their annual review sheets. An artist soars on updrafts, only to plummet into a black hole when the praise-winds die. The specific activity varies, but in each case our approval addiction centers on the thing most important to us. We peel back skin, baring our passion to the brutal and often inaccurate feedback of others.

Sensitivity to feedback increases according to its relationship with your sense of meaning in life. Students hang the hope of their future on teacher support. For the career-focused, approval of bosses and customers takes on a life-support role.

Objectively received feedback can offer valuable insights that help us improve and propel us toward our God-given goals. But when gratifying others' opinions becomes our goal, divine purpose gets lost altogether. As a post from John Maxwell's blog so aptly puts it, "You cannot successfully lead your team if you need your team to validate your self-worth."[8]

Personality Approval

My long-held belief that my father held bulletproof likability turned out to be a myth. He spent long hours crafting a sermon to underscore our

---

8. The John Maxwell Company, "Insecurity: The Leadership Flaws of America's Worst President," *John Maxwell on Leadership* (blog), September 6, 2012, http://www.johnmaxwell.com /blog/insecurity-the-leadership-flaw-of-americas-worst-president.

longing for heaven. I remember him explaining his point with passion, "There's no place like our eternal home with God our Father." Dad even covered a pair of thrift-store shoes with red glitter to illustrate his point. Before delivering the sermon, he beamed with excitement. I congratulated him ahead of time, praising the brilliant theme. But his work did not fall on approving ears. A parishioner filed a formal complaint against him for using *The Wizard of Oz* as an analogy. The incident provoked little response from district superiors, but it hurt at a personal level. Criticism always cuts us.

It seems my father is in good company, however. The Church of Christ railed against Max Lucado over doctrinal differences. In an interview to promote his book, *It's Not About Me*, Lucado stated, "I really gave up on trying to answer to or even please everybody else. I don't think we're called to do that."[9] Even Billy Graham, that icon of American faith, endured persecution from certain Christian groups.

Biblical examples of persecution and rejection include Joseph, Isaiah, Jeremiah, Hosea, Mary Magdalene, Peter, Stephen, and Paul, and that only scratches the surface of the list. Facing ostracism or death, early church members felt rejection's most intense heat. Seeking acceptance from their pagan neighbors would prove more than a little tempting.

Paul knew this when he prayed the Lord would "strengthen you with power through his Spirit in your inner being . . . to grasp how wide and long and high and deep is the love of Christ, and to know this love that surpasses knowledge" (Ephesians 3:16–19). Only one resource could equip them to resist the pull of buckling under such overwhelming

---

9. Bobby Ross Jr., "Best-selling Christian author declares, 'It's Not About Me,'" *The Associated Press* State and Local Wire, March 6, 2004, https://bobbyrossjr.com/2004/03/06/march-2006-the-associated-press/.

pressure. The same anchoring truth stands as our sole hope for protection today—the marrow-deep assurance of God's incomparable and soul-quenching love.

Validation Card

Copy the following biblical statements on an index card. Insert your first name or use the personal pronouns provided. Keep these affirmations with you as a reminder of your divine ID—an approved child of the Most High. Let your card-carrying status stand as evidence you don't need any further validation.

> I speak as a woman "approved by God to be entrusted with the gospel." I'm "not trying to please people but God" who is the only one able to examine my heart (1 Thessalonians 2:4).

> God has blessed me "in the heavenly realms with every spiritual blessing in Christ" (Ephesians 1:3). Before creation, the Lord had me "in mind, had settled on [me] as the focus of his love, to be made whole and holy by his love. Long, long ago he decided to adopt [me] into his family through Jesus Christ." God took immense pleasure in designing my life and wanted me "to enter into the celebration of his lavish gift-giving by the hand of his beloved Son" (Ephesians 1:4–6 *The Message*).

> I was chosen as part of the divine Christ-centered plan and marked with the seal of the Holy Spirit as a deposit that promises my eternal inheritance. "It's in Christ that [I] find out who [I am] and what [I'm] living for. Long before [I] first heard of Christ and got [my] hopes up, he had his eye on [me], had designs on [me] for glorious living, part of the overall purpose he is working out in everything and everyone" (Ephesians 1:11–12 *The Message*).

Empowerment Questions

1. At what age(s) have you struggled with approval-seeking behavior?

_____

_____

_____

_____

_____

2. Which of the approval issues have you struggled with in the past?

_____

_____

_____

_____

_____

3. Consider the extreme makeover list. Which biblical hero(es) do you relate to most, and why?

_____

_____

_____

_____

_____

4. Pray through Ephesians 3:16–19. How might this Scripture passage transform your need for approval?

_____

_____

_____

_____

_____

_____

5. Which approval issue causes you the most pain right now? Pray through releasing your need for human approval. Journal the gradual shift in your spirit as your heart's burden subsides.

_____

_____

_____

_____

_____

_____

Chapter 6

THE TRUTH OF CHRIST'S
APPROVAL

I ascended the concrete block stairwell with my gaze fixed on the narrow steps. I had to watch my sandaled heels or risk introducing myself as the Lucille Ball of Sunday school teachers. Accurate, maybe, but not the way I wanted to go in. A teen boy bounded downstairs and brushed past my arm, muttering some apology. I gripped the steel railing and gasped at his confident vault over the final third of the banister.

He stuck the landing too.

Ever the momma, my worries for his safety prevented me from offering any compliments on his acrobatic stunt. Instead, I warned him to be more careful.

He responded with a broad grin, beaming with all the marks of what many people describe as youthful confidence. Something I couldn't recognize from personal experience.

I quickened my pace, hoping to minimize my time in the stairwell's disaster risk-zone, and entered the second floor hall. Small windows peered from the sentry line of doors into the musty corridor. I strode to the first room. The frigid knob sent a shudder from my grip to my shoulder, but I entered with little hesitation.

Clad in shades of coal, the girls turned from their huddle at the far side of the room. And glared. Silence froze the air.

Until a broad-shouldered teen curled her lip. With a toss of her hair, she snarled at the youth leader standing among them and aimed a finger at me. "What's *she* doing here?"

The words skewered my core. It didn't matter that a fourteen year-old launched the dart. The shot plunged me back to my own youth. Not confident. Rejected.

Other young voices surged from memories of long ago and joined in to deride me in that moment. Once again, I was the little pauper child gazing through a picture window into the world of acceptable, lovable people where I could never belong.

Still reeling from the blow, I forced myself to speak my name in the present. To explain I had been called upon by the person in charge to help with this class. Even as I regained my composure, the impact of the girl's disdain continued to burn. My chest ached, as though a battering ram had slammed into my breastbone.

Deeper than appearance or performance, the most insidious type of shame lurks in the marrow of identity. We fear others will reject us, not merely for our looks or abilities, but for who we *are*. A desperation for acceptance surges into our conversations and lifestyle. A silent, yet haunting title—*unlovable*—compels us to seek approval.

Our culture pumps its media-bellows into the insecurities burning within our hearts. Magazine and Internet quizzes promise to identify and measure our acceptability. With all the scientific accuracy of a Magic 8-Ball, pop culture tests promise to categorize our personalities. Are you fashionable? Socially inept? What do your habits say about you? Don't tell me you haven't clicked on at *least* one. The evaluation grabs our attention because it pricks at a common insecurity shared by human beings.

Who am I, really? And will others accept me?

We long for human acceptance because we're designed for community. Our souls pursue relationships because a relational God created us in His image. The Lord's original blueprint mapped a flow of security and love from His Spirit connecting all human hearts. Fear didn't enter our interpersonal dynamics until sin broke our intimate bond with the Creator (see Genesis 3). Because we lost touch with whose we are, we also forgot *who we are.* Shame announced our exposure, sending us to duck and cover.

Christ paved the way to restored intimacy with God and peace with His children. Still, we struggle to live out the full benefits of our redemption. We know God loves us, but the voices of the broken world and the seductive whispers of our long-held insecurities compete for mental space. Unless we grab hold of our God-given identity, our minds will adopt the unhealthy suggestions encircling them.

People pursue self-discovery and personal development in hopes of erecting an identity that others will embrace. There is nothing wrong with becoming your best. Nor is there any crime in improving your social skills. But *if the main goal of reinventing yourself* is to please others, failure awaits. *No one* can be adored by *everyone.* Worse yet, you could miss out on the most fulfilling outcome of personal development—becoming who God intended.

Had I centered my identity upon Christ, I would never have placed human acceptance on a pedestal. Jesus told us, "If the world hates you, keep in mind that it hated me first. If you belonged to the world, it would love you as its own. As it is, you do not belong to the world, but I have chosen you out of the world. That is why the world hates you" (John 15:18–19). God promises love, but the world betrays our security.

It seems the best of us remain vulnerable to the fickle nature of society's approval.

A cavity in our hearts aches for merit. We long to feel loved. Yet, no matter how much affection we receive from other people, the void persists. We run from puddle to puddle, trying to fill our dried inner seas with a teaspoon. The needs of our soul are God-sized. Only He is big enough to meet our needs for love and significance.

Who I Am Says I Am

I am handcrafted by the perfect Creator. He sees my entire being and defines me as a very good creation. "God saw all that he had made, and it was very good" (Genesis 1:31).

I am created in God's majestic image. The Lord shaped me to resemble Him and breathed Himself into my essence. As a living reflection of my Father's likeness, I am blessed. "When God created mankind, he made them in the likeness of God. He created them male and female and blessed them" (Genesis 5:1–2).

I am wonderfully made. The Creator knitted each strand of my DNA, forming my cells, tissue, and features with intentional design. Long before my birth, he lovingly crafted my soul and orchestrated the days it would reside in these flesh-robes. The Ultimate Artist creates only wonders. None of His workmanship, not even the slightest detail, ever falls short of a masterpiece. "For you created my inmost being; you knit me together in my mother's womb. I praise you because I am fearfully and wonderfully made; your works are wonderful, I know that full well. My frame was not hidden from you when I was made in the secret place, when I was woven together in the depths of the earth. Your eyes saw my unformed body; all the days ordained for me were written in your book before one of them came to be" (Psalm 139:13–16).

I am a daughter of the Most High God, a divine princess. Jesus extends His nail-scarred hands, offering me a priceless gift—His name. Christ invites me to share His birthright. "Yet to all who received him, to those who believed in his name, he gave the right to become children of God" (John 1:12).

I am sanctified. Jesus spoke cleansing words into my soul. He invites me to remain immersed in His powerful Spirit. As long as I reside in His presence, we can conquer anything together. "You are already clean because of the word I have spoken to you. Remain in me, as I also remain in you. No branch can bear fruit by itself; it must remain in the vine. Neither can you bear fruit unless you remain in me. I am the vine; you are the branches. If you remain in me and I in you, you will bear much fruit; apart from me you can do nothing" (John 15:3–5).

I am chosen. From the dawn of eternity, while I remained a distant glimmer on time's horizon, God envisioned and chose me for a purpose. From the vast and spangled universe of life, He picked me. I was born neither by mistake nor happenstance into His family. I was selected for adoption because my identity as His daughter brings a smile to God's face. My Father adores me. He lavishes me with precious gifts of grace and wisdom. "He chose us in him before the creation of the world to be holy and blameless in his sight. In love he predestined for adoption to sonship through Jesus Christ, in accordance with his pleasure and will—to the praise of his glorious grace, which he has freely given us in the One he loves. In him we have redemption through his blood, the forgiveness of sins, in accordance with the riches of God's grace that he lavished on us. With all wisdom and understanding" (Ephesians 1:4–8).

I am God's precious baby girl, and He has a royal inheritance planned for me. The Spirit of Christ dwells within me, cooing with affection to the Lord from the depths of my heart. "Because you are his sons, God sent the Spirit of his Son into our hearts, the Spirit who calls out, '*Abba, Father*.' So you are no longer a slave, but God's child; and since you are his child, God has made you also an heir" (Galatians 4:6–7).

I am a significant part of Jesus' household, and He invites me to share in the family business. "For whoever does the will of my Father in heaven is my brother and sister and mother" (Matthew 12:50).

I am God's friend. He whispers the secrets of God's deep truths into my soul. Christ chooses me for an eternally significant destiny and equips me to fulfill it. God will give me whatever my Best Friend and I ask for together. "I no longer call you servants, because a servant does not know his master's business. Instead, I have called you friends, for everything that I learned from my Father I have made known to you. You did not choose me, but I chose you and appointed you so that you might go and bear fruit—fruit that will last—and so that whatever you ask in my name the Father will give you" (John 15:15–16).

I am crowned with glory and honor. No matter what anyone else says about me, no matter how anyone else treats me, I will not stand condemned. The Creator of the universe lifts me into His arms and esteems me among the heavens. The Lord redeems His servants; no one will be condemned who takes refuge in Him. Though my father and mother forsake me, the Lord will receive me. "When I consider your heavens, the work of your fingers, the moon and the stars, which you have set in place, what is mankind that you are mindful of them, human beings that you care for them? You made them a little lower than the angels and crowned them with glory and honor. You made them rulers over the works of your hands; you put everything under their feet" (Psalm 8:3–6).

I am the subject of His love songs, which blanket my soul day and night. Even when life's chaos overwhelms me and I struggle to see it, God pours relentless devotion over me. "Deep calls to deep in the roar of your waterfalls; all your waves and breakers have swept over me. By day the LORD directs his love, at night his song is with me—a prayer to the God of my life" (Psalm 42:7–8).

I am the object of God's undeterred love, and He draws me into His eternal embrace. "The LORD appeared to us in the past, saying: 'I have loved you with an everlasting love; I have drawn you with unfailing kindness'" (Jeremiah 31:3).

I am valued by God, treasured above all other works of creation. "Look at the birds of the air; they do not sow or reap or store away in barns, and yet your heavenly Father feeds them. Are you not much more valuable than they?" (Matthew 6:26).

I am a life-giving stream of God's Spirit. "Whoever believes in me, as Scripture has said, rivers of living water will flow from within them" (John 7:38).

I am engineered to shine as God's light for the world. "You are the light of the world. A town built on a hill cannot be hidden. Neither do people light a lamp and put it under a bowl. Instead they put it on its stand, and it gives light to everyone in the house" (Matthew 5:14–15).

I am precious to my Father. He attends to the fine details of my life, even the number of hairs on my head. "Are not two sparrows sold for a penny? Yet not one of them will fall to the ground outside your Father's care. And even the very hairs of your head are all numbered. So don't be afraid; you are worth more than many sparrows" (Matthew 10:29–31).

I am a coheir with Jesus Christ. He covers me with His righteousness and invites me to join His position as the chosen, beloved, delighted child of God. "Here is my servant whom I have chosen, the one I love, in whom I delight" (Matthew 12:18).

I am granted power and authority by Jesus to conquer evil and bring spiritual freedom on earth. "Truly I tell you, whatever you bind on earth will be bound in heaven, and whatever you loose on earth will be loosed in heaven" (Matthew 18:18).

I am ordained for a holy purpose. God sent me to be Christ's disciple. I am growing more intimately acquainted with God each moment. Jesus pours an endless stream of sweet God-knowing into my soul. I am drenched with His love. Jesus's deep wish is to fill me more with Himself. "Righteous Father, though the world does not know you, I know you, and they know that you have sent me. I have made you known to them, and will continue to make you known in order that the love you have for me may be in them and that I myself may be in them" (John 17:25–26).

I am beloved by Jesus and God, who graciously shower me with encouragement and hope. Christ sustains my heart and strengthens me for all I say and do. "May our Lord Jesus Christ himself and God our Father, who loved us and by his grace gave us eternal encouragement and good hope, encourage your hearts and strengthen you in every good deed and word" (2 Thessalonians 2:16–17).

I am united with the Lord in spirit. "But whoever is united with the Lord is one with him in spirit" (1 Corinthians 6:17).

I am empowered by Jesus Christ. He strengthens me to accomplish every task for which He calls me. "I can do all this through him who gives me strength" (Philippians 4:13).

I am a marvel of divine engineering. God prepared my life's purpose beforehand and crafted me in Christ Jesus to do good works with Him. "For we are God's handiwork, created in Christ Jesus to do good works, which God prepared in advance for us to do" (Ephesians 2:10).

I am securely wrapped inside of Jesus and destined to appear along-side Christ in the glory of His eternal kingdom. "Your life is now hidden with Christ in God. When Christ, who is your life, appears, then you also will appear with him in glory" (Colossians 3:3–4).

I am the temple of God's Holy Spirit, which lives and breathes within me. "You yourselves are God's temple and that God's Spirit dwells in your midst" (1 Corinthians 3:16).

I am an ambassador of Christ, and God makes appeals through me. "We are therefore Christ's ambassadors, as though God were making his appeal through us" (2 Corinthians 5:20).

I am raised with Jesus. God seated me with Christ in the heavenly realms. The Lord plans to show off His wealth of grace by how much He esteems me. "And God raised us up with Christ and seated us with him in the heavenly realms in Christ Jesus, in order that in the coming ages he might show the incomparable riches of his grace" (Ephesians 2:6–7).

I am completed and sufficient. All the fullness of Christ dwells in me, including His authority over evil. "For in Christ all the fullness of the Deity lives in bodily form, and in Christ you have been brought to fullness. He is the head over every power and authority" (Colossians 2:9–10).

I am secure. I have a firm position in God's kingdom. I belong to Jesus and have been sealed for my dignified status with the Spirit. I have even more blessings destined for me. "Now it is God who makes both us and you stand firm in Christ. He anointed us, set his seal of ownership on us, and put his Spirit in our hearts as a deposit, guaranteeing what is to come" (2 Corinthians 1:21–22).

I am the Lord's masterpiece in progress. My faithful Jesus will continue working good things in me until His perfection saturates the world. "He who began a good work in you will carry it on to completion until the day of Christ Jesus" (Philippians 1:6).

I am born of God and lovable by all His other children. "Everyone who believes that Jesus is the Christ is born of God, and everyone who loves the father loves his child as well" (1 John 5:1).

I am an overcomer. Victory over the world's darkness belongs to me. "For everyone born of God overcomes the world. This is the victory that has overcome the world, even our faith. Who is it that overcomes the world? Only he who believes that Jesus is the Son of God" (1 John 5:4–5).

I am found and adored. God ripped out his own heart and wrapped it in human skin to rescue me. With unfathomable love, God sent His Son to die in my place. Jesus knew He was my only hope. Christ shared the Father's deep adoration for me. Despite excruciating emotional and physical torment, He tore himself open as my doorway out of hopelessness and death. Jesus will always remain my love-destined way, truth, and life. "Jesus answered, 'I am the way and the truth and the life. No one comes to the Father except through me'" (John 14:6).

Empowerment Questions

1. When have you experienced rejection?

_____

_____

_____

_____

_____

2. In what ways have experiences with rejection affected your self-image?

_____

_____

_____

_____

_____

3. Which cultural messages have tempted you to focus on human approval? How might you resist this thought pitfall in the future?

_____

_____

_____

_____

_____

4. Consider the Who I Am verses on pages 64–71. Which verse resonates most with you? How might this verse help you center your identity upon Christ?

_____

_____

_____

_____

_____

5. Write the Scripture passages most relevant to you. Where might you post them to best change your mindset for each day?

_____

_____

_____

_____

_____

Chapter 7

PREVAILING OVER LONELINESS

After days inside the cavernous space of my home, the pale walls encroached with a chilling, dead stare. I struggled to motivate myself to work. My new online business required me to write new content several days per week, so my sluggish mood needed an immediate solution. Inspiration had fled my heart and mind. I fought to write each paragraph. I tried new vitamins and added protein to my diet. Extra caffeine failed to resurrect my creativity. I listened to webinars and podcasts, which cheered me for an hour or so. My work soon dwindled back to a dragging pace.

Isolation clouded my eyes from within. My self-image weathered to a grayed, haggish character. An inept recluse, confined to her dark tower and forgotten. My gait remained a trudge.

Up the stairs, back to my corner.

Alone.

A few months into my business, I decided to visit a creative group. After a three-hour drive, I joined the pre-meeting social hour. New acquaintances related their passions and stories. I loved the beautiful spirits filling that place. My heart leapt, eager to support their vision and fulfill my purpose. I gushed with ideas, and encouragement flowed.

Although staying the length of the meeting meant I wouldn't arrive home until after midnight, my energy level soared.

On the return drive, the key to invigoration dawned on me. I laughed at myself. Of course I felt better. I'm an extrovert. Engaging with groups of people recharges me. I had set myself up to work alone all day, every day. What on earth was I thinking? Instead of guzzling vitamins and caffeine, I needed to schedule regular fellowship into my week. Places to pour myself out as a blessing.

All hearts hunger for the soulful embrace of others. An introvert needs smaller, but more potent doses of connection. Extroverts, on the other hand, need a broader and more frequent supply. Regardless of our wiring, we are designed for relationship. All of us.

Without quality in-person relationships, isolation lowers mood and esteem. The problem comes because few of us access what we need. We believe the unlovable lies whispered to us in the darkness when no one else is there to counter the slander with truth.

Madness

Our minds, hearts, and souls starve when deprived of human contact. During the nineteenth century, a bizarre rash of insanity swept the American plains. Behaviors ranged from despair to violence. Known as "prairie madness," the phenomenon involved an alarming number of farmers and their wives who lost touch with society . . . and their minds. While some debate whether environment caused these psychotic episodes, modern scientists show increasing concerns over the damaging effects of isolation. NASA invested millions on behavioral health studies to identify and prevent psychological damage from long-term solo missions.

Regardless of our wiring, we are designed for relationship.

Suburb and city residents may live within shouting distance of neighbors, but loneliness can imprison us in the midst of a crowd. When emotional distance gapes around us, we feel trapped on a personal prairie.

Many of my counseling clients have expressed this sense of isolation. One woman's face sagged as she described the stream of posts on her social media networks. She declared her life bleak in contrast to the indefatigable happiness others appear to enjoy.

"Everyone else's life seems peachy," she said, "but mine has all the sweetness of raw kale."

I told her she wasn't as alone as she felt and explained the important distinction between *virtual* identities and real life. Many of us post our best and hide ourselves. We share cheery avatars that belie unshared broken hearts.

The despondent woman smiled, noting how much it relieved her to know others experienced seasons of kale flavor too.

Several teens have expressed feeling awkward in social situations. Though their fingertips dance easily through online interactions, their lips fumble with the forgotten art of conversation. Most didn't suffer from brain dysfunction or developmental delays. These kids simply lacked practice. Those who reached out to others got better at it with each attempt. Teens who refused to venture outside the virtual reality made no progress.

Our culture disconnects people. Healthy individuals slip into cyberbubbles and float away, detached as airborne islands unto themselves. Care and outreach diminish. People lose hope in true friendship and nail themselves inside the one-room cabin of isolated living. Like the madness of a past era, disconnection now spreads like a virus. The world has never been more connected.

Nor has it ever been lonelier.

Barriers and Myths

We need emotional intimacy to thrive. Lonely hearts feel something missing but struggle with perceived barriers. Loneliness distorts our outlook and makes it difficult to reach out and break the spell. It's difficult to see the truth from within the fog of our own thoughts. Inertia sets in, and our minds take up residence in the Dalí-like world of loneliness. We settle into a state of familiar discomfort, lacking the drive to change.

Self-fulfilling myths reinforce the prison tower of isolation. Acting upon the false beliefs causes situations that make the myths seem true. This cyclical thought distortion holds the lonely person in a self-defeating pattern. There are three main distortions created by loneliness—inadequacy, mistrust, and self-serving motives.

Inadequacy suggests something is wrong with *us*. We believe we can't connect. We doubt our ability to offer value to others. When we're feeling unsure of ourselves, transparency is the first thing to go. People who feel inadequate either pretend or withdraw.

Someone who copes with inadequacy by pretending may center herself in discussions, layering excessive words to feign expertise. She fakes confidence because she has none in her *true* self. In a desperate effort to connect, she drives away those she hopes to befriend. Others find her insufferable, which feeds her sense of inadequacy and fuels the pretense.

The person who withdraws to cover her inadequacy would tend to hover near an exit at a gathering, checking her watch with a frown. When approached, she mumbles and avoids eye contact. She overhears the whispering jabs at her apparent snobbery. She turns away to escape, desperate to be somewhere else. As the murmurs roil at her back, she wishes she could be *someone* else too. Her avoidance adds layers of brick to her tower walls.

Mistrust insists others will hurt us because something is wrong *with them*. We believe others aren't going to accept us because of a pessimistic view of human nature. Like many negative beliefs, this one often starts with a painful experience. Abuse. Bullying. Betrayal. Wounds fester with itchy assumptions about others to guard ourselves from repeating the trauma. If we don't allow ourselves to develop positive experiences, the isolation leaves us unable to heal. Instead of renewing our minds and hearts, we can choose to keep picking those rancid suspicions until they are raw.

A distrustful person looks for flaws in others. Since no one's perfect, the fault-finder is guaranteed to come up with a shortcoming every time. The person who expects betrayal refuses to share her best with others. Smiles elude her, and her posture and tone remain guarded. Bitterness grates her attitude and word choices. She rolls her eyes when others confront her excessive sarcasm. The tension knots her gut and muscles, tossing her through one restless night after another. Minor problems pique her frustration, and she snaps at the nearest bystander. When her disdain drives others away, she considers it proof of humanity's untrustworthiness.

The third distortion, selfish motives, might sound insensitive. Yet isolation will turn our thoughts inward if left unattended. For someone who exists as an island for an extended period, all things begin to flow through the filter of how it affects them, including connections with others. A lonely person who pursues relationships only to alleviate their emptiness becomes a parasite instead of developing healthy, balanced relationships. When someone views the primary purpose of connection as meeting their own emotional needs, the motive is self-serving.

While healthy people resist parasitic, one-sided relationships, predators allow the attachment as a means to take advantage of a vulnerable person. Abuse or rejection deepens the hunger. The self-serving efforts to draw life from others intensify in a destructive cycle.

The more we focus on our emptiness, the greater the void grows. As we gaze into the pit of our loneliness, our view darkens. On our own, we cannot see clearly enough to remove barriers and free ourselves from confinement. We need help to recognize the misconceptions and take action.

Solutions

The solution to loneliness is to break the toxic inward stare. Stop feeding the monstrous cycle of hopeless myths. Turn your focus upward and outward in a love that puts God first. Whatever we lack, we trust God to pour through us. A faithful heart reaches toward others with compassion. Whatever others might do, we trust God to have our backs. Whatever seems empty, we believe He will fill. If we respond to loneliness with love for God and others, our needs are met while we are sincerely pouring into others' hearts.

God shows us we have no need to protect ourselves. Pain will be there even if we live in distrust. We're no safer in our attempts to self-protect because our defenses don't guard us. They destroy our spirits. A broken heart mends inside a faithful spirit, however. God will transform the wounded into more beautiful children than they were before the wounds. We need not fear the dagger, the words, or the human frailty when God promises renewal on the other side of connections.

A child of God lays down her needs at the Father's feet. She expects her Father to provide and sets out on a mission to pour out her heart. A life of faith means we donate our cause, our vision, outward instead of seeking fulfillment. The more we turn our meaning toward service, the less empty we feel. It is the irony and the miracle of the jar of endless oil.

In 1 Kings, we find an ancient widow who chose to accept this sacrificial quest and become a divine heroine in God's miraculous story. God told Elijah to go to a widow who would supply him with food. Elijah found the widow at the town gate where he asked her to draw him some water. As she went to get Elijah something to drink, he also asked for the food.

> "As surely as the LORD your God lives," she replied. "I don't have any bread—only a handful of flour in a jar and a little olive oil in a jug. I am gathering a few sticks to take home and make a meal for myself and my son, that we may eat it—and die."
>
> Elijah said to her, "Don't be afraid. Go home and do as you have said. But first make a small loaf of bread for me from what you have and bring it to me, and then make something for yourself and your son. For this is what the LORD, the God of Israel, says: 'The jar of flour will not be used up and the jug of oil will not run dry until the day the LORD sends rain on the land.'"
>
> She went away and did as Elijah had told her. So there was food every day for Elijah and for the woman and her family. For the jar of flour was not used up and the jug of oil did not run dry, in keeping with the word of the LORD spoken by Elijah.
>
> —1 Kings 17:12–16

The Lord directed a starving widow to give up the last of her food supply. Preparing to watch a son die would sour any woman's mood. With gut-wrenching hunger compounding her grief, her willingness to draw water for a stranger might seem shocking. She follows her cultural mores of hospitality for the prophet's first request, but devastation and fatigue weigh her heart. His plea for food finds her at the end of social functioning. Her community has abandoned her, and she can no longer put on the mask of normal life. She lays out her bitter situation in protest—she's taking her meager food home for a last meal with her son. God should ask someone with more food to help this guy.

But this nameless widow made a remarkable decision. Contrary to all logic and natural inclinations, she offered everything in obedient outreach. And her sacrificial gift sparked a miracle that saved lives. In addition to the three people who survived on the endless flour and oil, consider generations of family descendants and the countless lives saved when Elijah prayed to end the drought.

Just as the Lord called the least-equipped widow in a famine-struck city, he also invites us to give our handful of flour. Like our story's hopeless woman, we must choose whether to dwell on our circumstances or obey His call. The widow could have turned away from Elijah and gone home. Had she heeded her own emotions and experience, her family history would have ended that day with tragedy.

We cannot experience abundance while choosing an isolative scarcity perspective. The answer to our emptiness resides in surrendering all to God's call for us to love one another. Our lives must be lived in loving outreach instead of fear. We hold back no dollop of oil, no sprinkle of flour. We listen to the Holy Spirit and share every last teaspoon he prompts us to divulge.

Anchoring our relational identity in our relationship with Jesus untangles the distortions born in loneliness. Faith rewires our connections to God, self, and others as a sustaining system of love. God loves us first. To the extent we receive His love, we can love ourselves, love God, and love others. Our hearts are not limited to what we can produce or what others can provide. Our part in the kingdom of love no longer consists of human island myths.

Christ's love dispels inadequacy. Faith allows His Spirit to fill us. The only sufficient love is the love of God. The devoted Creator can, and wants to, supply us with all we need for effective relationships with others. We no longer need to doubt our sufficiency. We are not limited to our own resources. Renamed by Christ as spiritual billionaires, when we trust in God and His love, we no longer need to believe ourselves vagrants.

Mistrust and self-serving motives find healing in the ugly beauty of grace. Someone had to show us we could—we *should*—do this hard and unthinkable letting go. So God sent His sinless Son. Jesus loved, mentored, and washed the feet of twelve friends, most of whom He knew would turn their backs on Him when He needed them most. He fed their souls and bodies, knowing one of them would sell Him to those waiting to torture Him to death. As he Hung with open gashes baking in the sun, Jesus struggled for enough breath to speak forgiveness . . . for the men who beat His body into mangled tendon strips on bone . . . for the friends who snored during His final prayer and ran away during His capture.

How did He let go of the need to self-protect with resentment? Jesus never entertained the illusion that bitterness would save his heart from pain. He knew where to place His trust—through men, past friends, and into God's hands. He didn't need to concern Himself with suspicion because He knew His destiny was to serve God regardless of man's frailty.

Because of our untrustworthiness, in fact.

He drew His friends—all of us—close to His heart in all the known risk factors because it allowed Him to be who God called Him to be despite what others might do. The eternal result of fulfilling God's purpose was worth temporary suffering. He had no illusions of a painless life, but He would not seek it instead of love. Love was worth the risk, and it would repay Him infinitely more than it ever took away.

This model applies to our lives too. We will be hurt. We will be disappointed. So in order for God to fill us with His fullness, we must first position ourselves in loving relationships and let it pour *through* us. In the love viaduct, we find blessings worth the risk. We become who God intends, more than we ever dreamed. And we find pain is a temporary part of life, as mortal existence is a temporary part of our eternal glory within a greater kingdom.

God takes the grisliness of our pain and makes it into a beautiful offering. Our ugly cry transforms into compassionate understanding for others. Our betrayal becomes Christlike forgiveness and faith. The grotesque beauty of grace, the loveliness of a crucified Savior, only happens when we surrender our mistrust and take up faith in a God who is big enough to deal with our suffering.

He binds our wounds and creates art from the scars.

Faith draws us out of insecurity's walls to share with other starving souls. Then we see God multiply the resources He provides. What we perceive as a risk, God knows as a miraculous opportunity for imminent heroines.

Battering Ram for Insecurity Walls

If loneliness and insecurity have imprisoned you, bludgeon your way to freedom and purpose. Look past the lie of inadequacy. No resource is too small when placed in the hands of the Creator who made the universe from nothing. Cite your inventory and surrender each asset, claiming your faith in "him who is able to do immeasurably more than all we ask or imagine, according to his power that is at work within us" (Ephesians 3:20).

What "handful of flour" might God use to bless others through you?

Spiritually: What truths have you learned or could you learn more about? Do you know your spiritual gifts? If not, take an inventory online (like www.freeshapetest.com) or at your church to discover them. Every Christian, no matter how new, has something to offer from the indwelling Holy Spirit.

Emotionally: Perhaps you've longed for a friend while the answer lies instead with becoming the neighbor someone else needs. The simple formula for friendship is to listen, prove trustworthy, and demonstrate compassion with respect.

Through your experience: Surrender your past, with all its scars, to the Redeemer. Allow Christ to craft beautiful ministry from your pain. The repurposing of our suffering vanquishes the enemy in the most elegant and perfect defeat. When we bare our scars to offer healing, we bear the image of Jesus and therefore represent the ultimate threat to evil.

With regard to time: Take a moment to pray with someone. Join a weekly volunteer group or study. Go to lunch with the new coworker who doesn't know anyone yet. Stop by a nursing home to read to those who don't get visitors. A sprinkle of shared time fends off waves of loneliness.

From your material resources: Find personal ways to bless others from your "handful of flour." Make dinner for a neighbor, pastor, or church member. Repurpose old blankets or clothes into items that could be used by the needy in your community. Help veterans' organizations fill donation boxes with magazines and books. Clear outgrown clothing from your closets and pass them along. Volunteer to distribute the items, when possible. Consider adding personal notes to each donation.

Through talents or sheer kindness: Do you sing or play an instrument? Are you tech-savvy? Do you have a lawnmower? Are you great at repair work? The abilities you take for granted could offer immense blessings

to others in your community. Look for needs among the widows of
your church, local hospitals and nursing homes, and daycare programs
for at-risk populations.

Empowerment Questions

1. When have you experienced loneliness?

_____

_____

_____

_____

2. What myths did you believe about yourself when you were isolated?

_____

_____

_____

_____

3. Which barriers or distortions have created obstacles in your life?

_____

_____

_____

_____

4. What step could you take to choose faith instead of obeying the limits of insecurity?

_____

_____

_____

_____

_____

_____

5. If all limiting beliefs were removed, where could you belong?

_____

_____

_____

_____

_____

_____

6. What might a redeemed mindset free you to do?

_____

_____

_____

_____

_____

_____

Chapter 8

REDIRECTING THE WHY

When he was three years old, curiosity manned the helm of my son's mind. His worldview centered upon a single question: "Why?"

My firstborn performed this classic echo with Olympic persistence.

He gazed at a thundercloud one afternoon as we stood under a carport. "Mommy," he began, his sweet voice edging upward. "Why does it rain?"

"When the clouds are wet, it rains." I wiggled my fingers to demonstrate a rain shower.

"But *why*?"

"To water the earth."

An eddy of windswept leaves rushed past our ankles on their way to the storm.

"Why?"

"Plants need a drink to live, and rain brings it to them."

Placing a hand on his hip, he widened his stance. "*But why*?"

I sighed as a downpour splashed mud onto the edge of the carport. "Because water on the earth evaporates and rises into the atmosphere," I said, knowing full well I was likely talking over his head. "In the clouds, colder temperatures cause the vapor to condense. The

water droplets fall to the earth as rain. This is known as the precipi-
tation cycle."

He nodded, his cherub lips pursed. "Oh," he said. "Okay."

Those who've raised a toddler might identify with my inward groan-
ing during those conversations. We'd just survived the "no" stage only
to run headlong into the challenges of "why." *Please let my patience
withstand this phase.* I assumed his resistance and questioning would
diminish with maturity. We all outgrow these petty stages eventually,
of course.

Or do we?

Though toddlers stop echoing "why" to their parents, resistance and
doubt don't drop from vocabulary after the age of three. Just like kids,
grown-ups question things. And the truth is often far above our heads.

Some questions remain outside our need or ability to understand.
We wrestle with trusting God to know all things when we do not. We
forget our identity does not depend upon our expertise but in his.

So when we turn to other sources for answers or His response fails
to satisfy us, we continue asking. "Why" persists in unbridled issues
of the heart and soul—an ultrasonic echo bouncing off the corners of
our mind, hammering the frame of our worldview. When we accept an
answer, we grab onto it with both hands. The explanation we choose
to believe, whether true or false, determines how we see the world and
ourselves.

My own why questions had been aimed in the wrong direction for
much of my childhood and beyond.

For example, when other kids didn't like me, I wondered why. Hor-
rible lies shimmered like dark mirages in the air. *They don't like you
because you're unlovable. And your parents only love you because they're
good people. No one else will ever accept you.*

Because I grasped at the shadows and believed the lie, it shaped how I saw other people and the world. I expected rejection and created a self-fulfilling cycle of it in my life.

The questions resurfaced time and again.

A few years ago, a why trigger evolved from years of publishing rejections. *Why are my writer friends getting published while I continue to fail? Why can't it be easier than this?*

Why not me, Lord?

I recognized doubts of my calling and myself but missed the darker side of my questioning. My attitude reflected little faith in God's goodness and sovereignty. Because of my skewed worldview, I wavered in my commitment to my calling. I lost motivation. I didn't feel like writing because I hadn't seen results. And I didn't understand *why not*.

"Why?" isn't always negative, but when laced with certain attitudes, it can distract us from fulfilling our Christ-centered identity. Look underneath the why to identify criticism, self-absorption, or comparison.

Three basic types of why exist: curious, self-focused, and soul-purposed.

The Curious Why

In its proper perspective, curiosity remains fairly harmless. Sometimes seeking a better understanding of the world helps us resolve problems with it. Curious why questions peer into others' behaviors, how things work, or what could improve.

Why do people . . . ?

Why does the world work like that?

Why don't we change this?

I'm personally grateful for the curiosity that swirled and grew in someone's brain to birth the automatic dishwasher. An automobile brings me closer to family, volunteer opportunities, and mountains. And I *strongly* appreciate the pacemaker that keeps my grandmother's heart beating.

An inquisitive nature can also be toxic if it takes on a judgmental tone. *Why won't that person drive the way I do? Why can't that idiot do what I want?* When criticism and complaint sour the question, it bears rancid attitudes toward others and disrespect for God's role. Judgment exists far outside our wheelhouse and remains God's responsibility alone.

Curiosity also poses a risk if the pursuit of knowledge becomes idolatrous. Ego and knowledge worship present sly temptations. Archaeological notes in the margins of my study Bible distract me during sermons sometimes, and I have to remind myself to focus on the spiritual message instead of looking up cross-referenced verses or reading historical details. This seems like a mild example, but it can lead to a very serious spiritual problem.

In the early church, a movement called Gnosticism involved the veneration of knowledge. This heresy suggested it was not faith in Christ alone but also education that drew people nearer to God. When anything takes Jesus' role, it becomes an idol. This risk applies not only to academics like me but also to experts in any field. Artisans, mechanics, or truck drivers could fall prey to the same trap with different bait.

The Self-Centered Why

When self-centeredness prompts the question, it veers in a malignant direction. I'm not talking about self-examination, which can benefit those who intend to take responsibility for problems. If a brief inner inventory motivates changed thoughts and behaviors, great. But many whys come from a toxic perspective. They are not action-oriented but paralyzing in their misery and fraught with bitterness, shame, or excuses.

Why me?

Why now?

Why not?

Why do I have to . . . ?

Why can't I?

Why do they get . . . ?

Why are they different?

Why don't they just . . . ?

In refusing to claim their potential, these why echoers see themselves as helpless. This pattern of blame and complaint imprisons their own hearts and minds. Clinical experts refer to this as a victim mentality.

I've worked with many victims in the course of my career. I've been preyed upon as well. But not all victims adopt a victim mentality. Nor do all those with this toxic mindset have a trauma history. Anyone can be subjected to crime, loss, or natural disasters. Healthy individuals choose to seek help and overcome circumstances. They make use of every resource, no matter how meager their supply. These heroines insist on a healing journey and often use their experience to help others.

My great-grandmother, Gladys, lived on a rural Illinois farm during the Great Depression. One afternoon, during a major hailstorm, her windows were broken. In those days, home-improvement stores didn't ship new panes in a few days. Nor did they offer credit card deals. So she faced gaping holes in the side of her house with no way to pay for repairs. Nothing to protect her children from animals, insects, or icy wind. And it would stay that way into the unforeseeable future.

As she gathered the hailstones from among the glass shards, Gladys sent her kids to the neighboring farms with a calm instruction. "Invite everyone over. We're having an ice cream party."

A victim of a major financial crisis, she could have focused on her lack of resources, her hopeless circumstances. She *could* have asked, "Why me?"

Instead, she looked past her crisis to the shared plight and assessed her opportunity to bless others—a rare commodity of ice had descended upon her home. And neighboring families could use a bit of cheer during this season of hardship. Damaged windows remained, but the warmth of her attitude strengthened them to get through stark times.

I love that story. Instead of responding as a victim, my great-grandmother chose to take action as a divine heroine. She inspires me to transcend the default reactions so common to human nature and instead turn window-breaking stones into sweet ice cream.

"Why?" robs those with a victim mentality of power. "Why me?" maintains their plight should not belong to them, therefore they have no responsibility for changing it. "Why now?" inspires procrastination. "Why not?" suggests tragedy removes accountability. Since life has not been good to me, I should be permitted to do or have whatever I want.

While we'd all prefer to deny such mindsets, traces of these attitudes creep into our thoughts more often than we'd like to acknowledge. The self-focused why remains a common part of our human frailty. And our enemy attacks us with it all the time. What's the first thought to pop into your mind when supervisors choose someone else for a promotion? When your car jolts as colliding metal bumpers screech into your ears? When doctors offer painful treatment as the best option?

Like all of us, I'd like to have the life of my dreams paved out in front of me. One I can see and understand, with no potholes. I'd rather enjoy perfect health and a padded bank account than sickness—even a cold—and a red-numbered checking deficit.

Wouldn't you?

But prosperity fails to test character. Or strengthen it. I have grown from the moments I didn't get everything the way I wanted and had to trust God with the future. Not that my first responses showed a saint's faith, of course. If I'd been spiritually mature to begin with, I wouldn't have needed God to nurture and fortify my spirit.

In 2011, I read expert reviews as I strode through my fourth writing conference. Red scrawl glared up from the last page of my manuscript submission. *This is not exciting.* No suggestions for improvement. Just criticism. Again. The envelope crinkled in my tightening grip as my gut churned in the bile of why.

Why me? Why not me? Why can't I get the easy success others seem to enjoy?

My prayers shot off like silent rockets as I stormed to the hallway. "I don't think you know who you're calling here, God. I'm not Noah. I don't have this kind of perseverance."

His response floated into my mind. "So . . . *you* don't think *I* know who *I'm* calling."

I huffed. "Fine. You're God, so I suppose You know everything. Like who You're calling." My nostrils flared. I rolled the manuscript into my fist. "But I want You to know, I don't like how this is going."

God waited a few minutes before He responded.

My breath cooled and deepened. I trudged into the cafeteria and stood in line.

The Lord brought an image to mind. Nailed to a raw, splintering black post, Christ's feet hung at eye level before me. Thick callouses lined the soles and wrapped the edges to meet a smattering of bruises. Blood streamed through encrusted earth, from his ankles to his quivering toes.

He said, "Tina, if I only asked you to wash my feet, would you do that for me?"

Tears blurred my view as I gazed through the cafeteria window at the lake, where a cross stood between the shoreline and the building. "Yes, Lord."

Attitude shift.

I'd committed my life to Jesus. But I still needed to choose to live for Him instead of living as though it's all about me.

I wish I could say that moment marked the last selfish thought to enter my mind. It didn't, of course, since the enemy persists in his attacks. But it marked a turning point. I don't wallow in self-focused whys any more. I reach for the Lord to get me out of the piggy mire as soon as I sniff out the selfishness of it.

Because if we stay too long, we'll forget we have work to do. In seeking our desired path, we could miss out on an amazing life that infinitely surpasses our imagination—the life of *His* dreams.

When focused inward for extended periods, we can lose sight of the importance of living for something greater than ourselves. Doubt creeps like mildew into the closed mindset. Ugly notions seep into the windowless walls of our heads.

"Why should I?"

"Why can't I get what I want instead of doing this?"

Maintaining the balance between healthy soul checks and outward focus might seem impossible. Humans, in fact, cannot manage holistic wellness on our own. We all need Christ's help to get through our life struggles.

Or help others through theirs. You can't tell what others need by looking at them through envy lenses. Or comparison goggles. Or entitlement attitudes.

Jesus said, "You hypocrite, first take the plank out of your own eye, and then you will see clearly to remove the speck from your brother's eye" (Matthew 7:5).

Sometimes it benefits us to take a brief self-examination to find out what can be improved. The only beneficial reason to look inward is to correct an issue, not to deepen the problem by obsessing over what's wrong with us. If we get paralyzed in the negatives we find, our self-absorbed why can mire us in is shame. The common saying, "The windshield is bigger than the rearview mirror," lends itself to this principle. A hopeless focus on past or present mistakes prevents forward movement.

The Spirit didn't discipline me to anchor my life in shame but to remedy its needs and move it in the direction of His purpose.

The Spiritually Purposeful Why

Same words. Altogether different whys.

Why do people . . . ?

Why does the world work like that?

Why don't we change this?

Why me?

Why not me?

Why now?

Why not?

Why do I have to . . . ?

Why are they different?

A Christ-centered attitude transforms our questions as we commit to a purpose higher than curiosity or self. The spiritually purposed query seeks to resolve others' needs. It shifts our role from victim (or outcast) to servant. It drops the comparisons, and seeks outreach through empathy and compassion. When we align our questions with God's purpose, it sets us free from the common strongholds of focusing too much on our own plight.

A divine heroine pursues action-oriented conclusions. The spiritually purposed why invites God to respond with His resources. Our questions seek to determine the needs around us and what God can do through us to respond. We aren't limited to human wisdom for strategy or our own resources to carry it out. The Spirit equips us to respond to the needs around us. We then can partner with God to help further His purpose to bless the world. His plan outshines any we could devise.

For example, I wondered why I suffered rejection from a self-absorbed point of view. Now I pray for God to use my experience to free others from the prison of shame. I asked God why He would call me to years of writing when no one seemed interested in reading my words. But my reason to persevere revealed Himself—the one who suffered unimaginable torture to save me. If He asks, isn't that why enough for anything?

Some whys don't resolve with a vision or even a clear answer. In reality, many of the true answers lie outside our ability to understand. Explanations of fate rest beyond human comprehension. Human nature rankles at the unknown. Many of us settle for a lie we can manage instead of trusting an unseen God to govern what we'll never understand. When given a choice between God and knowledge, the first people on earth shirked the trustworthy Creator for a chance at divinity. The lie of humanism continues to plague us today.

Faith, by definition, involves the continued existence of something we can't fully perceive. Believers trust in an all-knowing God even when He doesn't share all the information. Some look forward to getting their answers in heaven. But the *desire* for answers is unlikely to follow us into eternity. Once we find ourselves in the presence of amazing love and surrounded by glory beyond our imagination, none of the why questions will matter. We'll experience the goodness of who God is along with the joy of our eternal identity as His heroines, and that will be enough to answer our doubts.

From Victim to Victorious

Examine your thought patterns and list any self-centered why questions that often tempt you. Note the situations that tend to trigger these thoughts.

Why me?

_____

_____

_____

_____

Why now?

_____

_____

_____

_____

Why not?

_____

_____

_____

_____

Why do I have to . . . ?

_____

_____

_____

_____

Why can't I?

_____

_____

_____

_____

Why do they get . . . ?

_____

_____

_____

_____

Why are they different?

_____

_____

_____

_____

Why don't they just . . . ?

_____

_____

_____

_____

Why (other)?

_____

_____

_____

_____

Transcend the victim's role by rejecting helplessness. For each previous thought, clarify your responsibility and God's power. Rewrite spiritually focused whys on a sheet of paper. Keep the list handy to fend off the temptation to default toward a victim's mindset.

Spiritually purposeful why examples include: Why might God use me to change this? Why not me? Why might God use this to change me? Why might God have placed me in this situation at this time?

Empowerment Questions

1. Which toxic why questions do you find yourself asking?

_____

_____

_____

_____

_____

_____

2. Have you ever focused on a spiritual why? If so, what benefits did you notice?

_____

_____

_____

_____

_____

3. Pray through your list of toxic questions. Replace each one with a redirecting, spiritual why.

_____

_____

_____

_____

_____

4. How might a Christ-centered attitude change how you experience life?

_____

_____

_____

_____

_____

5. How could a spiritually centered mindset improve your relationships? How might spiritually focused why questions improve your impact upon others?

_____

_____

_____

_____

Chapter 9

FREEDOM FROM BITTERNESS

Palmetto bushes and scrub pines outnumbered people in my childhood neighborhood in Central Florida. I walked alone most weeks, strolling for miles along the house-freckled woods. My off-brand Keds crunched through the brush beside our dirt road.

Ragweed and shoulder-high thickets loomed at the road's dead end. I decided to explore the canopied lane to my left. I kicked a tangerine-sized rock ahead of me. The tumbling stone stirred a dust plume into its wake. Beyond the haze, a dark form appeared at the bend in the road.

A bear?

I froze as the dirt veil settled. In the strain of high alert, silence squealed in my ears. Our gaze locked, the beast ventured a step closer—wrong gait for a bear.

Growls erupted, identifying the beast as an enormous dog. I swallowed the catch from my throat and spun on my heels, then shot off down the graveled road. The scratch-whoosh of galloping paws gained behind me. I fought through the air, elbows pumping.

Over half a mile later, I dared to glance back. No sign of the predator. I scanned the area just in case—houses, cars, any hiding spots for a canine monster. I brisk-walked and jogged, pressing the dregs of my energy onward. Once inside my house, I leaned against the door and locked it.

As much as I loved the beauty of that canopied lane, I never walked that way again. Dogzilla marked the only time an animal chase threatened my life, but my heartbeat still rises at the sight of *any* unleashed canines—monsters, ankle biters, and everything between. I've fled at full throttle from short-legged dachshunds.

When someone threatens me, my brain's natural response is self-protection. Which is great, if it's a bear or Dogzilla. I need an instinctive reaction when deadly jaws snap at my face. Pausing to consider how to diplomatically resolve our differences might not work out so well for me.

After a perceived danger leaves, my brain imagines ways to prevent a future attack. Block the doors. Bar the windows. Dig a trench fitted with sharpened stakes around my property. Because, you never know. The predator—or others like it—might attack again.

The brain makes no distinction between life threats and relational threats, however. And until I shift my mind from defense mode, it remains on high alert for as long as I consider myself at risk. I've judged the threat, and now I stand at arms. I'm just protecting myself. Or so my resentments have led me to believe.

Our perceived self-protection doesn't work as we expect. What we think protects us is actually killing us. We might as well have slammed ourselves inside an iron maiden. As it has been often noted, unforgiveness is like drinking poison and waiting for someone else to die.

The toxin proves most deadly when the person I refuse to forgive is me.

In my self-enmity, I searched for someone to blame and targeted myself. Though facing a merciful judge, I continued to hold myself under scrutiny. My sense of identity—the very thing from which I should draw nurture—soured with shame.

Ain't That a Shame

One of the usurper's favorite tactics involves perverting the blessings God offers His beloved children. He substitutes a destructive counterfeit in place of God's original gift. In a subversive move, he redirects us from God's gift of conviction to the cancerous alternative of shame.

God provides His children with conviction as a protective blessing. He implanted a conscience in our nature to apprise us of wrong choices. Believers enjoy the additional power of the Holy Spirit's wisdom to advise us against potentially devastating mistakes.

Conviction functions much like our physical nervous system, which gives vital feedback to the brain. Touch a hot stove burner, and nerves relate the danger using pain signals. You can then react to protect yourself from further harm. Stop. Withdraw your hand. Treat the wound.

And don't ever do that again.

When the Holy Spirit alerts us to a problem, our mind has the opportunity to respond. The Lord suggests a different course of action to preserve our soul's optimal functioning. Stop. Treat the wound.

And don't ever do that again.

A key test to differentiate shame from conviction is this: if we fail to heal and move onward, we're rooted in shame rather than conviction. After removing ourselves from destructive behavior, shame can paralyze us. We clutch our sore hand and drop to the floor crying. *Ah, I am such a fool for touching the hot stove. How could I be so worthless? I'll never touch anything with this hand again.*

The example seems silly. No one would refuse to use their hand just because they had burned it, would they? So then what about a seared heart? Inner aches can last longer than third-degree burns.

Shame is not of God.

The Bible clearly distinguishes shame from conviction. "Godly sorrow brings repentance that leads to salvation and *leaves no regret*, but worldly sorrow brings death" (2 Corinthians 7:10, emphasis added). *Godly sorrow is conviction*. It leaves no regret. Shame douses us with regret like cheap cologne. Satan distorts the perfect gift of conviction into worldly sorrow, or shame. Unlike the forward movement God intends, shame stops us dead in our tracks, bringing spiritual death.

But God's design redirects us to obtain healing in order to move forward in a life of freedom and peace. Then the Holy Spirit pours healing water over our wounds and advises us toward life-giving activities.

> Praise the LORD, my soul, and forget not all his benefits—who forgives all your sins and heals all your diseases, who redeems your life from the pit and crowns you with love and compassion.
> —Psalm 103:2–4

Toxic Traps

Shame and resentment are two flavors of the same poison. The guilt-ridden refuse to forgive themselves while a bitter heart refuses to forgive someone else.

Whether toward others or ourselves, the toxic effects of bitterness threaten with similar destructive patterns. The more severe the wound and the longer the grudge remains, the deeper the poison delves into a person's psyche.

Bitterness paralyzes the soul and suffocates the body, impairing all of our interactions. When afflicted with resentment, we lose touch with life. The heart we tried so hard to protect grows ill along with mind, body, and soul.

Unforgiveness is literally poisonous. Anger and stress release chemicals that bolster a quick response to threats, but prolonged exposure to these chemicals harms the body. Unresolved anger or resentment leads to increased stress, which can cause several health problems, including headaches, digestion problems such as abdominal pain, insomnia, increased anxiety, depression, high blood pressure, skin problems such as eczema, heart attack, and diabetes.[10]

In addition to poisoning our bodies, bitterness impairs us on more levels than we ever expected—destiny, identity, and even our faith.

1. Destiny

Resentment influences how we perceive others. We render snap judgments to guard ourselves. Anyone who reminds us of *that* woman, *that* man, or *those* kinds of organizations cannot be trusted. Fear exaggerates and convinces us of doom. But all dogs won't harm, nor will all women in small groups or all men who drive trucks. In our avoidance, we isolate ourselves from the very individuals designed to pour spiritual value into our lives. Prejudgments rob us of blessings, both to be given and received.

Bitterness contaminates how we treat others. Complaints surface more often than we realize. Nerves grow more sensitive every month. Acquaintances and strangers trigger negative reactions in seconds. We might not recognize our poisoned body language, attitudes, and voice tone, but our sourness will be clear to everyone else.

2. Identity

Resentment creates a self-fulfilling prophecy of victimization. We unknowingly present ourselves as abuse targets and misanthropes.

---

10. "Stress and Your Health," MedlinePlus, NIH: US National Library of Medicine, accessed February 19, 2019, https://medlineplus.gov/ency/article/003211.htm.

Well-balanced folks don't enjoy the company of those who harbor grudges. Instead, we draw predators into our lives by limping on the outer edge of the herd in our unforgiveness or self-hatred. The cycle repeats itself. And until we identify the tower walls keeping us in circular paths, we don't understand why.

Bitterness also dooms us to become more like our enemy. The dark side of unforgiveness is its essential rejection of God as the sovereign judge. If we claim ourselves as judge, we're ultimately declaring ourselves a rival to Jesus.

It's as though we declare to the Lord, "Okay, Jesus, scoot on off that throne. I'm taking Your job as judge because I can do it better than You."

3. Faith

Unforgiveness thumbs its nose at the Savior and turns its back on the flow of grace. We rail against mercy for the villain, but that same condemnation blocks our ability to receive mercy. Then the blocked flow sours and rots our hearts. When we live outside of grace, the transforming power of Christ lingers outside our hearts. We can't both withhold and enjoy mercy in the same soul.

Toxic Resolutions

Like bulky accessories, bitter vows often accompany unforgiveness to further hinder our freedom. People etch *shoulds, musts, nevers,* and *always* into human-sculpted, false security. This form of self-protection declares we hold power over the future. We deny our helplessness by aspiring toward a sense of control. But vows intended to guard the heart can become its prison.

I'll never . . .

No one else will ever . . .

I will always make sure . . .

The Scarlett O'Hara quote from *Gone with the Wind*, "As God as my witness, I'll never be hungry again," sounds like a typical resolution. Toxic vows aren't always this melodramatic or memorable, however. Many occur before our sixth birthday and drift into the deep recesses of memory. Consulting a Christian therapist, pastor, and spiritually mature friends can offer insight when introspect comes up short. While prayer remains the ultimate guide, the Scriptures do not call us to keep our prayer requests to ourselves.

> Is anyone among you in trouble? Let them pray. . . . Let them call the elders of the church to pray over them and anoint them with oil in the name of the Lord. And the prayer offered in faith will save the sick person well; the Lord will raise them up. And if they have sinned, they will be forgiven. Therefore confess your sins to each other and pray for each other so that you may be healed. The prayer of a righteous person is powerful and effective.
>
> —James 5:13–16

Solutions

Whether you suffer from resentment of others or yourself, there are two steps to take that will dismantle your bitter stronghold and set you free. You must dig up the resentment's core and rid yourself of it.

Exposing bitterness is the first step on the journey to freedom. Irritability often points to a triggering thought. List the moments when you tend to get touchy. This will help identify sensitive areas. Try to recall when those feelings first occurred. Explore underlying thoughts and beliefs.

The next step in the process involves ditching the baggage holding us back. Bulky resentments and toxic resolutions keep us from crossing the threshold to peace. Jesus stretches out His arms to unburden us of resentment and other self-protective myths. He stands ready to take the weight of our fears, wounds, and anger. We need only ask for His help and take the step of choosing to forgive.

Prayer serves as a priceless tool in both steps of this process, since it connects us to the ultimate resource for exposing resentment. That said, it requires two things of us: we must submit ourselves to the Holy Spirit's searchlight and be willing to listen to His guidance.

A life of faith requires trusting Jesus as Lord. In order to experience grace, we must lay our judgments of others at the feet of the true judge. He works with us on the journey of surrender and release.

Forgiveness and surrender of bitter vows serve to detoxify the mind, body, and soul. The offender no longer takes over our thoughts as though he deserves rent-free space in our minds. Tension diminishes, relaxing muscles and improving organ function. Neurochemistry swings into balance when stressors of resentment no longer cause strain. Releasing idols and abiding in Christ allows us to enjoy the fullness of His blessings and grace.

Forgiveness does not involve letting a sinner off the hook. We're simply acknowledging they belong on a bigger hook. It is not in our job description to judge or deliver spiritual justice. And the one in charge, we proclaim, does His job with glorious perfection.

Forgiveness also does not equate with reconciliation. These two processes remain distinct. God requires forgiveness in all circumstances but leads us toward reconciliation when appropriate. *In some circumstances*, reconciliation puts innocent people at risk. It wouldn't be wise to invite a violent, unrepentant criminal as a houseguest. In other situations, reconciliation serves God's plan for blessing the offender and us. To know the difference in the two, we need prayer and mature Christian counsel to help us discern when to renew broken relationships versus when to offer forgiveness only.

Don't misunderstand me. Forgiveness with reconciliation does not mean we have to restore instant trust in those who have betrayed it. We should only trust people as they prove to be trustworthy. But we should also offer opportunities to build trust in small increments, which allows us to accept and heal while offering the offender time to stabilize character growth.

Keep a person's limitations in mind. You can still love and forgive someone who remains imperfect. But know where they can be trusted and where they cannot handle the responsibility. For example, you can love your dear old aunt with advanced Parkinson's disease. However, asking her to carry a tray of fine crystal stemware into the dining room may prove an unfair expectation. Don't press a person to perform something too far beyond the state of their character development. Instead, help repentant friends by offering small opportunities to demonstrate success. This allows you to remain free from bitterness and yet avoid setting loved ones up to fail.

But what if the person you most need to forgive is *you*? Forgiveness of self often seems more challenging than letting go of bitterness toward others. Still, no matter how difficult it appears, don't let yourself believe it can't be done. With God's help, anything is possible, which is good to note because in the battle against self, divine intervention is a must-have resource.

Another benefit of self-forgiveness is that it allows us to receive love and grace *from Christ* and involves similar steps to forgiveness of others. First, identify the offenses or flaws you resent. Take each one on a mental journey to Golgotha. Imagine wearing a paper crown as you march up the hill. Visualize yourself standing at the foot of Jesus'

Cross. Remove the crown, declaring surrender of your perceived right to judge yourself. Set the crown and your self-indictments in the puddle of Christ's blood at the base of the Cross. Breathe deeply, praying to receive grace and love, as you watch the paper dissolve into Jesus' blood. Listen for those awesome words that quaked the earth.

"It is finished."

Then, imagine Christ appearing before you in resurrected form. He takes your face in His hands and smiles.

"I made you. I have always loved you. I can renew you as a new creation. Do you believe in My love?"

Agree with Him, or let Him remind you of the Cross.

Imagine that He says, "Let My love heal your heart, renew your mind, and refresh your spirit." Then imagine Jesus embracing you. "One day at a time. When the accuser tempts you to think poorly of yourself, remember Me. Remind yourself how much I love you. Enough to suffer, to die, and to pursue you all this way."

Like the forgiveness exercise listed at the end of this chapter, you might need to repeat this activity. The enemy will continue to attack your esteem and worth, tempting you to return to old habits of self-loathing. Expect it and be ready to reject the lies. Ask others to pray for you as you go through the process of releasing shame and self-resentment. A list of Christ-esteeming Scripture passages can also aid your defense when the enemy attacks you with self-deprecating thoughts.

If you need to forgive others, the following Forgiveness Journey could lead you to much-needed freedom. The Forgiveness Journey process came to me while working with a client. Sometimes the words of counsel the Holy Spirit gives through me disappear from memory within seconds, but not this time. This journey has brought peace to many subsequent clients. That's my hope in sharing it with you.

If your forgiveness journey involves abuse or severe trauma, please invite a counselor or mature Christian to support you during the process. Depending on the nature, time, and severity of the wound, each step can take up to several months. Allow the necessary healing to saturate your spirit without giving in to impatience. Only, please don't give up on yourself or on the power of forgiveness. Keep your eyes on the Redeemer, who longs to crown you at the finish line.

Tactical Strategy: The Forgiveness Journey

Step One

Ask Jesus to come with you to confront the offender in your mind.

Step Two

Confront the offender in your mind. Holding Christ's hand for support, declare what the offender did wrong and how it hurt you. Grab the offender's hands, as though you were to handcuff them.

Step Three

Place the offender's fists in Jesus' hands. Take time to process how Christ heard your cries. Remember Jesus' presence to care for and support you. More than anyone in the universe, He's got your back. Remind yourself of God's ability to serve justice. Meditate upon the hands into which you're submitting this wrongdoer. Use a list of God's sovereign attributes, if necessary.

Step Four

Remove your hands. Leave the offender in Jesus' grip. This step begins the faith phase of the journey. Choose to trust Jesus. The choice precedes the emotion.

Step Five

Walk away, leaving the offender out of your mind and under Christ's custody.

Step Six

This one often takes the longest to reach. Pray a blessing upon the offender. Sometimes action accompanies this phase, but the change in attitude remains the most significant element. The ability to demonstrate compassion proves the process of forgiveness is complete.

Empowerment Questions

1. Do you harbor bitterness toward anyone?

_____

_____

_____

_____

_____

2. In what ways have you resented yourself?

_____

_____

_____

_____

_____

_____

3. What is the difference between conviction and shame?

_____

_____

_____

_____

_____

4. Pray for the Lord to reveal ways in which shame has held you back from experiencing the fullness of freedom in Christ. How might your life be different if the effects of shame were erased? Who else might benefit from your newfound freedom?

_____

_____

_____

_____

_____

5. What next steps will you take toward freedom from bitterness and shame?

_____

_____

_____

_____

_____

Chapter 10

REAL HEROINES, NOT BABY DOLLS OR HIM-POSTERS

Her platinum hair matched my downy toddler curls. Smooth, seashell-pink skin a shade more perfect than mine. With rubbery lips pursed and eyes fixed wide, she wore an eternally dumfounded expression. Baby Doll went everywhere with me, as though we were meant to rub off on one another. My grip thinned away layers of her hair. Smudges bruised her stain-sensitive skin, and words put upon her became lasting tattoos. Baby Doll had no special name, but her blank stare and vulnerability offered my first impressions of what womanhood might mean.

I later exchanged Baby Doll for Barbie, whose sapphire gaze and pouty lips insisted I should befriend and mimic her. Her physique presented an impossible standard of feminine beauty, and she required a male counterpart to complete her. I modeled my doll play after soap opera plots featuring women as vicious manipulators or perpetual victims of romantic tragedy.

During all this doll play, while my fun, extroverted father voiced his dreams and pursued them, I struggled to see who my mother was. Ever the quiet one, she juggled full-time jobs, household management, and childcare. I'd never doubt her faithfulness as a good parent, for she studied all the resources she could gather and worked long hours to care for our family. Though Mom later said she'd wanted to stay home *with us*, her many responsibilities and the trend of circumstances redirected me to spend most of my time with dolls and imaginary characters.

I devoured tales like *Sleeping Beauty* and *Snow White* in which a woman's security hinged upon her beauty's capacity to win a male rescuer's attention. While fairy magic left me spellbound, I sorrowed over the impossible distance between my isolation and happily ever after. A girl without charm, I fell short of the highness mark. My doughy flesh balked at squeezing into Barbie's shape. Other kids' slander marked me inside like the inky bruises on Baby Doll's skin. I helped tattoo my own heart with a peasant's scrawl—*unlovable*. No one would want to rescue a less-than-princess.

My influences soon broadened to include news reports and contemporary history lessons, which introduced contrary female role models. Some women rejected all things dainty or soft. Fists raised, the militants wore boxy, unflattering garments and chanted against the evils of men. Along with bra-burning mantras, extreme feminism demanded neutralization of both genders for the ultimate cause of equality.

The call for fairness wooed my soul, and the notion of strength resonated with my fiercely independent nature. I craved courage and fortitude but feared what I must sacrifice for feminism. Was it wrong to love poetry? To sigh at the sunset? To prefer feminine clothing? What if I *liked* jewelry? What if I *enjoyed* styling my hair?

I feared I would fail my gender and prove too weak to qualify as a roaring woman. My heart longed to be beautiful while my soul yearned to stand strong. I wondered if both were even possible in one human shell. By the time I entered high school, it occurred to me I sought to become something I couldn't define. I decided to research what designates a female as the ultimate woman, and if a heroine could be both strong *and* lovely.

It was then that I peppered the hallways with my one-question survey: "What does it mean to be beautiful?" I got a different answer from each person asked. As a generation, we stood—each one of us—equally confused.

The nebulous qualities of womanhood grew more perplexing with motherhood. Desire to nurture my newborn treasure pulled me homeward. At the same time, the lure of an education and respected career reeled me away with promises of significance. I should be the best possible wife, provider, mother, neighbor, volunteer, housekeeper, supermodel, citizen—a thousand "shoulds" tugged my priorities. My heart seams ripped in the middle. While I found myself understanding my mother more than ever, I still didn't know who I should be.

For such a common human experience, it's amazing how lost and alone we feel in the uncertainty of who we are.

Mine was not the only generation to misunderstand how to define womanhood, nor was my mother's or her mother's. The characteristics of femininity have eluded us since Eve and her husband chomped their way through a piece of fruit and out of God's ideal.

Godlessness torqued us off course in so many ways, including our sense of identity as women. We have veered so far into the wasteland of humanistic arguments, we seem doomed to a dumbfounded state. No one here knows whether the lasting smudges on a girl's skin mark her as a less adequate female or if our vulnerability should be accepted. People cannot clearly state beauty's meaning, if it serves a purpose, or whether women should cultivate it. Nor can we deem an accurate measure of a woman's strength—comparable to a man's, derived from a man, or unrelated to men altogether.

Across cultures and within their subsets, humans continually rewrite the qualities of identity and gender. Some even reject the concept of gender altogether, as though declaring it nonexistent could magically summon peace in a gray realm of androgyny.

In the turbulent sea of murky opinions, two resources offer us an anchor. We can examine the data verified by science and study the reality scrawled out for us by Truth Himself.

Science verifies that women and men are *not* the same. In terms of physiology, an abundance of gender distinctions range from skeletal structure to mammary glands. Even at the microscopic level, chromosomes identify the rest of a body as his or hers. Our design clearly reflects an intended difference. But *sameness* isn't necessary for *equal significance* in the eyes of our Creator.

To get to the root of our design, we must examine our origin before eating the poisonous fruit. God sculpted man and woman in His image (Genesis 1:26–27). After establishing our identity in relationship to God, the creation record then delves into detail about how our engineering with regard to one another, specifically the opposite gender.

God didn't need to pluck a rib from Adam to form Eve. He could have made her independently of man's DNA. But the Lord created two genders from one body for the purpose of supportive relationship. He sculpted us to fit together as a whole unit comprised of distinct, complementary pieces. Family offers our finite human minds an intimate means to glimpse our relational God's nature.

To fully reflect His triune image, the master artist sculpted a family model of separate, mutually supportive personalities. Father, Son, and Spirit complement, fortify, and perfect a singular entity of love. One person of God never diminishes the significance of another, yet Scripture continually demonstrates each part of the Trinity lifting up the others.

For this reason, the Creator did not scalp Adam to make Eve a head-master. Nor did God scrape her from man's heel to weave a woman-doormat. Instead, the Master Artist sculpted her from a bone that guarded his breath. As theologians put it, "She was not made out of his head to surpass him, nor from his feet to be trampled on, but from his side to be equal to him, and near his heart to be dear to him."[11]

God's intent to reveal Himself to us through creation shows up in the words of Scripture. The original word used to describe the woman as a "helper" is *ezer*. Scholars explain, "It is clear in the biblical text that at creation, woman was not intended to be subordinate to man, for the Hebrew word *ezer*, normally translated 'helper' (Genesis 2:18), is frequently used of God (e.g., Psalms 30:10; 54:4) and does not imply subordination."[12] Women bear the image of Father God as lovingly supportive yet powerful members of His beloved community.

A closer look at the sculpting of men and women reveals one of my fears has root in ancient truth. Sacrifice is, in fact, a necessary part of fulfilling divine identity. Woman was made from a man ripped open. She would then dislocate bones to birth offspring for the completion of family. Before her first child, however, humans broke faith with their Creator. Yet He knew sacrifice would remake us in His image. The Son ripped Himself open on the Cross to invite *ezer*, the Holy Spirit to dwell within us as an even more intimate way of knowing and relating to Father God.

The New Testament affirms the ideal status of gender equality, restored from its fallen state when Christ redeemed the world. "There is neither Jew nor Gentile, neither slave nor free, nor is there male and

---

11. Robert Jamieson, Andrew Robert Fausset, and David Brown. *Commentary on the Whole Bible* Harrington, DE: Delmarva Publications, 2013.

12. Paul J. Achtemeier, Harper & Row and Society of Biblical Literature. *Harper's Bible Dictionary* (San Francisco: Harper & Row, 1985).

female, for you are all one in Christ Jesus" (Galatians 3:28). This equal footing before God doesn't offer us a clear definition of our identity as women. It fails to resolve our dilemma of roles and responsibilities. In the taffy-pull world we face, who then are we meant to be?

I must mention a certain role model who may stand as the most despised woman of the Old Testament. Centuries of gals have greened and turned violently ill when reading her vitae. While I could mention a few female friends who astound me, this lady surpasses them all. She holds such a high bar, we tend to wish she'd just stop it already. Have you, like me, ever studied the superwoman of Proverbs 31 and felt ready to give up on being female?

With every talent and resource at her disposal, the "wife of noble character" (v. 10) resembles the ultimate comic book hero. She's got everything from wealth to an endless skillset. The beast-chick gets up at dawn and her lamp never goes out at night. If she never sleeps, it's no wonder "beauty is fleeting," right (v. 30)? While dominating the market with her textile business, she also profits in real estate, agriculture, and international trade. Boss Lady doubles as Domestic Goddess and manages to beat the local politicians in popularity. To top it off, she gets crowned Volunteer of the Year. Even her kids "call her blessed" (v. 28). Now, while I'm on pretty good terms with my grown sons at this point, I have yet to hear them spring out of bed in the morning to praise my character.

If her arms weren't so strong (v. 17), I'd have wanted to punch her. That is, until I discovered the truth behind this fabled woman.

Her standard seems impossible to live up to—because it *is*. She was never a real person, nor was her account meant as a canon for leveling shame. Her attributes aren't a checklist of requirements we must pass to qualify as acceptable women. Proverbs 31 shows faith-centeredness impacting a wide spectrum of feminine potential. As a devotional author wrote, "The crown of the woman's wisdom isn't her charm or her beauty or even her ability to 'get things done.' It is her fear of Yahweh. This relationship with God guides all of her actions. If we live to define ourselves by a task, or even a role, we'll fall short every time. It's God's work in us—through Christ—that defines us."[13]

Despite the patriarchal trends in ancient culture, the Bible records an astounding list of divine heroines. Each presents a unique character and role in the forging of kingdom ever-afters. From warriors and leaders to princesses and mamas, we see a broad variety of beauty and strength. But none model Christian femininity as a plastic doll or male imposter.

Sarah and Esther, both royally titled and renowned for surpassing beauty, made history as pillars of faith during times of uncertainty. Far from plastic, each of them overcame vicious trials and demonstrated character more radiant than their outward appearances.

These were not the only women whose faith made them victorious leaders. Jael (Judges 4:17–22) slayed an enemy commander. With more grit than the most seasoned soldier, the nomadic woman's hospitality skills served her the opportunity to drive a tent peg through a slumbering giant's skull. With surpassing grace and fortitude, Deborah led the entire Israelite nation (Judges 4—5). She demonstrated extraordinary prowess in her role, proving just as proficient with government as in spiritual leadership.

Rahab, known as a prostitute, stood against her community to save her family and aid God's people (Joshua 2–6). She committed her life to the redefining God, and He wrote her name in the genealogy of Christ (Matthew 1:5). Abigail's brave confrontation with

---

13. John D. Barry and Rebecca Kruyswijk, *Connect the Testaments: A One-Year Daily Devotional with Bible Reading Plan* (Bellingham, WA: Lexham Press, 2012).

David (1 Samuel 25) rescued her from the doom of her marriage to an overbearing fool and joined her instead to a king after God's own heart.

The Bible includes academic gals, ministers, and businesswomen too. Jesus praised Mary of Bethany for choosing to learn as a student at his feet (Luke 10:38–42). Miriam (Exodus 15:20), Isaiah's wife (Isaiah 8:3), and Anna (Luke 2:36) are mentioned among those with prophetic calling. Priscilla and other women held leadership roles in the early church (such as Junia in Romans 16:7). Dorcas, a textile businesswoman, spearheaded charitable ministry. She had such profound impact Paul raised her from death to continue her work (Acts 9:36–43).

Wives and mothers also made historical impact with their spiritual strength. When God's anger raged against Moses, his wife Zipporah intervened and saved his life (Exodus 4:24–26). After Hannah's heartfelt, believing prayer, the Lord granted her an extraordinary son (1 Samuel 1). Samuel transcended eras of leadership from judge to the prophet of kings. Paul commended Timothy's mother and grandmother for their sincere faiths and spiritual influence (2 Timothy 1:5). Mary humbly surrendered to divine motherhood despite the risks and scandal (Luke 1:38). She nurtured love in her arms while persevering hardships with courage and strength.

So as a woman, I am the mystery of God's image wrapped in flesh—at once soulfully beautiful and fiercely strong. In femininity, I whisper life-giving beauty into the world like the breath of the Word in creation. As a supportive side to my husband, children, and siblings, I offer the Spirit's wisdom as it is poured from God through me. I also roar like my Father, protective of the breath of my family's life against a prowling enemy.

I reject the plastic standards of soulless damsels. Let the dolls and their markings burn in the trash heaps. I also refuse to let militants wrest the poetry from my heart. I'll not surrender all things soft, lest I fail to become my true self through loving sacrifice.

The world has no right to define my soul.

Embrace Your Authentic Heroine Essence

List the myths of femininity you have believed. Declare your commitment to reject these cultural misnomers.

I reject the notions of:
>   Helplessness
>   Masculinity as the only type of strength
>   Style preference as the definition of femininity
>   Unmarried women as incomplete individuals
>   Seduction as an appropriate form of feminine power
>   Roles in the home or workplace as validation of femininity

Embrace your unique essence as a feminine hero in the kingdom of God. Consider your spiritual gifts, personality, influence, and all manner of aspects specific to your nature. Include the aspects that honor how the Lord created you and may use you to glorify his purpose. Refuse to compare your definition as a heroine to anyone else's, for you have your own warrior's name and role.

I am soulfully beautiful in the following ways (e.g. artistic, culinary, nurturing, spiritual gifts):

_____

_____

_____

_____

I am fiercely strong in the following ways (e.g. stand up for the helpless, prayer warrior, athletic, persevering through trials, protective):

_____

_____

_____

_____

_____

Empowerment Questions

1. How have you defined femininity or womanhood in the past?

_____

_____

_____

_____

_____

2. Have you ever modified your perception? If so, how?

_____

_____

_____

_____

_____

3. What expectations of women have you struggled with?

_____

_____

_____

_____

_____

_____

4. If you could have lunch with a woman featured in the Bible, who would you invite? What would you ask her?

_____

_____

_____

_____

_____

5. How might the female characters of the Bible encourage us as modern Christian women?

_____

_____

_____

_____

Chapter 11

CLOTHED WITH DIGNITY
AND STRENGTH

ate morning sun glared through my dorm room's cracked blinds. In the sliver of floor space, I wracked my gaunt torso through more than one hundred sit-ups—the first of my two daily sets. I wriggled skin-tight denim over jutting hip bones. As many of my friends did, I laid back on my bed and used a wire hanger to zip my jeans.

Cute equaled small. Pretty meant tight-fitting—as though a girl were only worthy of notice if she were minimized and shrink-wrapped.

With a ponytail band, I transformed a silk tank into a stylish half-shirt, gathering the hem up at a bulging rib. More importantly, with my abs bared I wouldn't be tempted to eat more than thirty-five calories. I dashed out of the building wielding a rice cake and diet soda.

Midday humidity simmered over the paved walkway to my first class. I'd hiked more than half the mile's trek when an approaching guy hailed me. I squinted through the haze at his unfamiliar face as he veered to station himself squarely in my way. And he asked if I worked at some breast-au-rant.

My growled "no" proved insufficient.

He insisted, confident I must be an objectified grease-server. My fingernails dug into my palms as my fists tightened. I don't remember if I *actually* hit him. But I'll never forget how much I *wanted* to punch his teeth through the back of his head. Whatever I said or did, he did not cross my path again.

Some would say I deserved his assessment. They'd allege I'd dressed scantily and therefore wanted to be seen as a sexual commodity. I can assure you with all ten knuckles I wanted no such role.

I yearned only to be beautiful, acceptable, lovable. With intense effort, discomfort, and even starvation, I sacrificed deeply in hopes of achieving good enough. But I didn't realize my skewed means of seeking acceptance had unwittingly leached away dignity and identity. Inch by creeping inch, who I was meant to become was being stripped away.

Like so many other young women, I didn't see a clear boundary to distinguish beautiful from baiting. Or recognize how such a small thing as scant outer wrappings could strangle my spiritual design. The world doesn't teach us to share the glow of inner value but instead schemes us into displaying our vessels until our clay surfaces are marketable for use.

One stroll through the mall's up-and-coming racks tells the modern story of an industry's role in dressing down the female gender. Fashion trends continue to invite us to wear ribbons and declare them a celebration. We're easily deceived into joining the party of wearing less to win acceptance among the pretty. Sexy trends have crept in and taken over children's departments, as though insisting we dress our toddlers to please pedophiles. While all of us love to feel lovely, we don't always see the insidious ways revealing styles undermine us.

In our quest to present ourselves worthy of acceptance, sometimes we unwittingly tag ourselves for quick sale. As though this vessel were some kind of merchandise to be ogled, handled, or owned. Young girls seldom realize their flesh hangs like meat before multiple generations of conditioned, wolfish eyes. Culture imprints the objectification of women onto young and old men alike, who leer and salivate as they grade each packaged cut of game.

Women are not the sole prey in this assault on spiritual worth. The same evil targets both genders at once, pitting us against one another. Newborn sons look up at their mothers with unadulterated love. As soon as their toddling feet venture beyond this maternal gaze, culture's dragon-like lies breathe full into their faces. From television cues to overt social pressures in class and locker rooms, the demand to dominate and objectify women persists.

Some guys resist the crowd and grow into heroes. Others click their way into the snares of addictive sexual behaviors. The entrapped boys might pray for escape. On their difficult road to freedom, they must also battle the deceptive consequences fashion has draped over the women around them.

Men cannot take the full blame for the social demeaning of women. We join the attack by putting one another down. How many of our own gender cannibalize those who fail to measure up to the smallest size, pull off the skimpy fads, or bare thighs with a gap?

Never mind how ludicrous these standards prove. Should we enlarge our knees until they exceed the girth of our legs in order to have a thigh gap? Are we expected to carve away all the muscle tissue permitting us to walk? We risk intestinal disorders, nerve damage, and internal infections when strangling our bodies with shapewear.[14] By whatever means, that unnatural shape makes an awkward, bow-legged stance. On a sexy pair of stilettos, no less. Teetering on wishbone legs could impair a heroine's ability to function.

------

14. Rebecca Adams, "Spanx and Other Shapewear are Literally Squeezing Your Organs," *Huffington Post*, January 20, 2014, https://www.huffingtonpost.com/2014/01/20/spanx-shapewear_n_4616907.html.

Women can hardly stand under the weight of cultural pressures stacked against us. In our confusion, we take aim at one another and lose sight of our true destiny. The enemy pits sisters against sisters, men against women, heroines against folks of either gender they could otherwise help rescue. We live in a world bent on decimating our identity and value, where evil hides its agenda behind many thin veneers.

Overcoming degradation proves an all-too common struggle. One in five women report they have been raped at some point in their lives, but these are the few brave individuals, the small fraction who raise their heads to speak out and represent a submerged iceberg of undisclosed assaults.[15] The US Department of Justice estimates only 30 percent of rapes are documented with law enforcement authorities.[16]

These figures don't include other types of molestation. A 2011 study found 38 percent of employed women experienced sexual harassment in the workplace. Disclosures of such attacks and denigration have recently begun to break into public awareness.[17]

Culture scoffs at the significance of harassment, at once urging us to dress sexier and blaming us for how we're treated. Even when celebrities reveal their demeaning experiences, both genders of our society question the validity of their claims. The same audiences who admire and attempt to emulate actresses are quick to target them as responsible for the behavior of those who mistreat them.

---

15. National Center for Injury Prevention and Control, "Sexual Violence: Facts at a Glance," Atlanta, GA: Centers for Disease Control and Prevention, 2012. Available at https://www.cdc .gov/ViolencePrevention/pdf/SV-DataSheet-a.pdf.

16. "Raising Awareness about Sexual Abuse: Facts and Statistics," The US Department of Justice, accessed October 25, 2018, https://www.nsopw.gov/(X(1)S(pk22zrti0zsu4khnzbmkgpfh)) /en-US/Education/FactsStatistics?AspxAutoDetectCookieSupport=1#reference.

17. National Sexual Violence Resource Center, "Sexual Violence and the Workplace," Atlanta, GA: Centers for Disease Control and Prevention, 2013. Available at https://www.nsvrc.org /sites/default/files/publications_nsvrc_overview_sexual-violence-workplace.pdf.

Sexual abuse, the ultimate degradation, drives the lies about a woman's value even deeper into victims' minds. The violating nature of molestation and rape defiles our sense of spiritual purity and worth. The experience itself does enough damage to our identity and esteem. To intensify the effect, perpetrators often add slanderous hisses and twisted notions of purpose into the ears of their prey. *This is all you're good for,* the villains suggest.

Whether the lie is spoken aloud or not, we often believe it at some level. Women of all ages and races endure the related aspersions we live within, yet few of us recognize our commonness as victims of slander. The deceit flows around us with such a common presence, it might as well join the fluoride added to our drinking water. Women swallow this guile without recognizing we've poisoned our own spirits. Fashion, harassment, and violation reverberate echoes of a prevalent demeaning message: a woman's only worth amounts to the world's dismissive view of her as flesh.

Let's stop joining hands with the liar behind this campaign and stand together for the truth about our value.

In no way do I expect women to mummify themselves in shades of gray muslin. Respecting our true value implies no requirement to chuck style into the trash can. The Creator spangled divergence into the universe and sculpted his imaginative DNA into each of our spirits. God embellished the whole of creation with an array of magnificent colors and varied textures. Scripture doesn't outlaw accessorizing to reflect our individual personalities. A full palette of colors, fabrics, and fun ways to configure them can reflect the beautiful diversity of God's family. As the Father employed a plethora of imaginative shapes and artful configurations in His artwork, He certainly offers us the freedom to demonstrate spiritual personality in our vessel-decor.

While a creative masterpiece swirls with stardust, chirps a million songs, and cascades from mountainsides around us, many fail to see its divine craftsmanship. Regardless of our efforts, there will always be those who fail to see divine worth crafted into our souls. Some will see God in us while others remain blind. Our responsibility is merely to express our true nature. And that is more than good enough.

We need only do our best to ensure our outer wrappings don't impede anyone's view of our spiritual value.

Character anchors image. With a Christ-centered esteem, a woman's individual style emanates from her soul. God-confidence allows her to stride without fear of under-exposure. She no longer feels compelled to fulfill the world's wolfish appetites. Nor does she need to concern herself with comparisons to other heroines. She is "fearfully and wonderfully made" (Psalm 139:14) and "called according to his purpose" (Romans 8:28). Free to be her truest, unique self, a divine heroine focuses on the source of her everlasting, radiant design. And it certainly isn't in her flesh.

Proverbs 31:25 says, "She is clothed with strength and dignity; she can laugh at the days to come." As divine heroines, we no longer need to swallow the world's deceit. We look within ourselves to the indwelling Christ and discover His antidote to the lies. Our esteem comes not from our flesh but from the blood of our Savior.

Jesus, who tore His body to become a garment for us, invites us to wear His image. He offers to replace our stained wrappings and their insulting tags with His righteousness. With love Himself as an outermost garment, our resplendent beauty transcends any world standard. A divine heroine bears the elegant loveliness of reflecting God's character.

> I delight greatly in the LORD; my soul rejoices in my God. For he
> has clothed me with garments of salvation and arrayed me in a

robe of his righteousness, as a bridegroom adorns his head like a priest, and as a bride adorns herself with her jewels.

—Isaiah 61:10

Our spiritual value, the strength of our inner beauty, marks the center of our true worth in Scripture. Our identity and mission is truest and most beautiful when aligned most closely with God's. As His daughters and ambassadors, we represent Christ to a lost, hopeless world. Those mired in perilous darkness could find a glimmer of hope if able to see His light when they look upon us. If His truth is obscured by layers of worldly flesh-focus, the lost will see only a reflection of their own quandary.

Optimizing our soul-sparkle isn't about shame mongering or legalism. Instead, we must purify the wellspring of grace within us. Divine beauty involves an inside-out regimen. Who we understand ourselves to be in Christ directs how we present ourselves to the world. If we're secure in our Christ-identity, our every outward expression will show His confidence and peace.

Sound impossible? As our unfortunate predecessor Eve found, human-centered efforts to achieve God-ness wreak epic failure. The serpent coaxed her to consider the beautiful, forbidden fruit. His forked words tickled her ears, "You will not certainly die . . . For God knows that when you eat from it your eyes will be opened, and you will be like God" (Genesis 3:4). On our own, striving to become "like God" *would* be unthinkable and disastrous.

Thanks to our Savior, we don't ever have to accomplish anything by ourselves. Jesus promised, "If you remain in me and I in you, you will bear much fruit; apart from me you can do nothing" (John 15:5). We have "the help of the Holy Spirit who lives in us" (2 Timothy 1:14) and a copy of His Holy Word "so that the servant of God may be thoroughly equipped for every good work" (2 Timothy 3:17).

The indwelling Spirit guides the minds of those who prayerfully attune to Him. As we focus on God and listen for His direction, He can steer us toward words and actions that complement our best features. Consulting His Spirit and Word together uncovers the secrets to help us rock the divine look. As Scripture tells us:

> Therefore, as God's chosen people, holy and dearly loved, clothe yourselves with compassion, kindness, humility, gentleness and patience. . . . And over all these virtues put on love, which binds them all together in perfect unity. . . . Whatever you do, whether in word or deed, do it all in the name of the Lord Jesus, giving thanks.
> —Colossians 3:12, 14, 17

Some might doubt their ability to pull off His multilayered style. What may seem like a complex fashion statement simply deserves closer examination and practice. So let's break down the pieces of our warrior-princess wardrobe.

Compassion rims an everyday outlook with the gilding of grace. The divinely accessorized soul lifts her eyes from her personal agenda and puts on a new perspective. Christ's love-lensed glasses allow her to consider how others may feel. Her heart aches to respond to the needs of her neighbors because she has adopted the "look" of his eyewear.

Kindness wraps our hands and feet in lustrous silk of *agapaō*, or love in action. Once our hearts see with compassion, kindness answers the needs with action. We do not wear the barbed gloves and shoes of codependence. Poor boundaries cut off circulation, grip others' responsibilities, and cripple growth. But kindness allows us to live out true empathy through healthy, smooth interactions.

Humility brands our spiritual wardrobe with the ultimate Designer's glorious signature. The grotesque tatters of self-denigration often get mislabeled as holy garb. Authentic humility never involves denying our identity as craftsmanship of a glorious maker. Esteem centered on Christ allows us to stride with His perfect symbiosis of divine confidence and loving humility. As servants of grace and heirs of glory, His label equips us to lift others up *without the need to put ourselves down.* As Philippians 2:5–9 says, "In your relationships with one another, have the same mindset as Christ Jesus: Who, being in very nature God . . . humbled himself by becoming obedient to death—even death on a cross! Therefore God exalted him to the highest place and gave him the name that is above every name."

Gentleness cushions our steps with peace. Others see our buoyance and serenity as great contrast to the uptight who lack spiritual insoles. We can deal differently with others because we trust in the loving Father who orders our steps. Gentleness is "an inwrought grace of the soul . . . in which we accept his dealings with us as good, and therefore without disputing or resisting . . . a condition of mind and heart . . . commended to the believer is the fruit of power."[18]

Patience gowns us with petal-soft fabric and caresses our skin with the King's adoration. With our souls wrapped in His secure embrace, anxiety no longer pricks shivers onto our hearts. Christ's comfort dresses us to glow with beautiful smiles. The snarls of impatience no longer contort our faces.

---

18. "Meek, Meekness—*Vine's Expository Dictionary of New Testament Words,*" Blue Letter Bible, accessed October 25, 2018, https://www.blueletterbible.org/search/Dictionary/viewTopic .cfm?topic=VT0001785.

Love descends from heaven to cloak our shoulders as divine princesses. Our *agapaō* robes complete the ensemble to distinguish us as perfect models of the Christ-look. We cannot emulate our Savior without this essential garment, for love defines true God-ness. And no radiance outshines the presence of a soul rich in love.

In Jesus name, the Word deploys us to wear His likeness in the world. Jesus confers His royal glory upon us with the mission to shine at the darkness. Our lips eat and drink for Jesus. We speak and act and react for love Himself. The hearts of our vessels no longer serve flesh but throb and live for the name of our Savior and King.

We can shrug off the world's slanderous rags and put on our priestess robes. Let's lift our heads high, sisters. The King crowned us with a title no one has the authority to redefine. We're outfitted for a holy mission to dispel the darkness, and nothing can outshine the stunning elegance of a divine heroine, clothed with dignity and strength.

A Heroine's Battle Garb

List ways you plan to enhance each part of your warrior wardrobe.

Compassion

_____

_____

_____

_____

_____

Kindness

_____

_____

_____

_____

Humility

_____

_____

_____

_____

Gentleness

_____

_____

_____

_____

Patience

_____

_____

_____

_____

Love

_____

_____

_____

_____

Empowerment Questions

1. Read 1 Corinthians 15:53. How can you apply this Scripture when choosing what to wear (inside and out)?

_____

_____

_____

_____

_____

2. Romans 13:14 encourages you to "clothe yourselves with the Lord Jesus Christ." How could you apply this concept through practical means in your life?

_____

_____

_____

_____

3. What might you change to improve your Christlikeness?

_____

_____

_____

_____

4. Which of the spiritual garment layers do you struggle with most?

_____

_____

_____

_____

_____

_____

5. In Luke 24:49, Jesus promises the Holy Spirit to His disciples by predicting they will be "clothed with power from on high." Pray for the Holy Spirit to empower your growth as you take steps to layer on the garments of a Christ-centered self-image.

_____

_____

_____

_____

_____

_____

Chapter 12

VALID COAT OF ARMS

U nforgiving white glared from my surroundings as I ventured onto the obstetrician's scale. The balance slammed awry and echoed down the linoleum corridor. The black platform shimmied under my swollen, unfamiliar form. I reached out to steady myself, but the nurse scolded me.

She slid those counter weights further. And further. Raising a brow, she scrawled the numbers onto the file. I peered over the page to see if the records had set a figure to reflect my inner state.

Unbalanced. Unrecognizable. Unsure who I had become.

Before I could read the data, the nurse drew the file to her chest. I doubted the medical record could offer me a sense of the self I lost.

After eight years of attempting control through starvation, I could no longer claim this body as mine. Flutters protested within my abdomen—a dependent life shifting me into something—perhaps *someone*—else. But still blighted. So unworthy. What sort of mother would I make?

I stumbled off the scale and followed the nurse down a frigid hallway. With a brisk clop-clop, she led me past offices walled with achievements. Like those everyone once expected of me. A tear slipped down my cheek and disappeared as swiftly as my lost scholarship. No longer the academic. My chin drooped. If only the yearbook could edit my title to read most *un*likely to succeed.

I entered the exam room where a folded bit of paper awaited me on the counter. I was asked to strip off my clothes and somehow cover myself with those few feet of tissue. The wall clock tisked at me. No matter how I tugged the impotent wrapper, *I* wasn't a fit. Shivering, I perched on the edge of the table. And waited. Haunting thoughts of my *un*-ness breathed chills over my soul. If a newborn or husband would just say he loved me . . .

Could their words render me lovable at last?

Years passed. Lower digits beamed from the scale. A framed degree adorned my wall. A pile of greeting cards documented the coveted "love you." Yet none of those things erased the *un*-ness etched like a cursed signet onto my identity.

I researched parenting techniques and followed the experts' steps, desperate to paste "great mom" over my coat of arms. At the same time, I strove to please my husband in hopes of earning the badges of "wanted" and the ever-elusive "lovable." Others' approval shifted like stickers on an oiled surface, however. Refusing to stay in place, their validation buckled, and my unlovable crest peeked through.

I sought to paint over my armor in hopes my appearance could mark me acceptable. I plastered cracks and blasted bulges. Forced my veneers to match acceptable lines. Layers of cosmetics, diligent exercise, and restrictive dieting streaked and faded over my surface.

A master's degree promised to cover more of the shield. But empty space soon glared from the earnings corner. If I could only achieve a respectable income. A significant career title. Accomplishments to decoupage "worth" onto my esteem. I layered award upon award, yet wondered how many more I needed to earn the badge of *enough*.

As John D. Rockefeller allegedly put it, "just a little bit more."

From the identity of "un," I could never achieve or be enough. None of the world's validation stickers could hide my heraldry's sinister engravings. Like many women, I had defined my identity with all the wrong standards.

Women often accept this cursed coat of arms unwittingly. None of us intends to etch our lives with *un*-ness. Yet our enemy vandalizes our identity through the pressures and instruments of this dark world. Immersed in shady culture, we buy marred armor as-is. As long as we cower in the enemy's shadow, we take ownership of his insults.

We measure ourselves on unreliable scales. Our eternal souls accept judgments based on the clay bodies in which they're camped. Temporary roles and inconsistent affections define us. And the achievements wrought from years of sweat and sacrifice gain fading stamps of validation.

"The prince of this world" (John 14:30), or as we call him by name Satan, established culture's terms for acceptance as a means of sabotaging our identity. The worldly measures of significance lure us as unwitting participants in our own demise. Before we know it, we've sought our standards from the enemy and adopted the wrong heraldry.

In the murky middle earth between flesh-dwelling life and heaven, an authentic coat of arms can easily get lost. As divine heroines, we're left squinting at the graffiti marring our shields. We wonder at the question echoing across time, since long before the dark ages.

"Who am I?"

In medieval times, a coat of arms protected its bearer by identifying the warrior in battle. After the fight ended, survivors could collect the shields and immortalize the lives laid down for their king. In a similar way, God-given identity guards our hearts and minds during the war against the ultimate enemy. The shield of faith immortalizes our affiliation with Christ long after our time on the battlefield ends.

Instead of the world's standards, the Lord commissions us to bear His image. This divine coat of arms reflects Christ's power, allowing us to gleam before all who observe our combat. As we lay down our lives on the battlefield, God honors us.

Divine heroines surrender all, but only to their King. The motto of our crown demands complete sacrifice. The Spirit overthrows all other defining powers that govern our identity. No other merit badges take priority over him. We live to please the King alone, and He is pleased with a surrendered heart rather than results of our efforts. In exchange for our life, we gain victory over death.

Only the Lord of lords can grant such an inheritance.

Medieval militants had to be granted a coat of arms by a ruling monarch to be able to legally use it. This old ordinance relates to a timeless spiritual law. *Only* the King of kings has the authority to confer our true identity. The Lord issues eternal patents to secure our significance. No one has the right to take or modify what God declares upon our heraldry.

We remain free to lay aside our divine coat of arms. Without recognizing our self-sabotage, we may choose to wear the rags of a slave to earth's standards. As women, we often identify ourselves with all the wrong status symbols—appearance, relationships, accomplishments. The quest for these paper merit badges exhausts us. All the while, our eternal heraldry gathers dust in the cellar of forgotten thoughts. It takes great deception to convince us to trade patents of royalty for tatters of shame.

The prince of this world conspires to disarm and destroy us. His strategy employs sleight of hand and visual distraction. Glittering temptations dazzle our eyes and draw our focus from their sinister consequences. Like in his oily sales pitch to Eve, he barters tangible charms in exchange for our spiritual sources of strength. We give up our faith shields for cardboard stage props. He knows a warrior cannot fight in the flimsy armor he sells us through daily pop-up ads. Appearance, affection, and achievements fail to galvanize our identity. If we remain vulnerable in an insecure sense of self, he gains the advantage over us.

> Be alert and of sober mind. Your enemy the devil prowls around like a roaring lion looking for someone to devour.
>
> —1 Peter 5:8

Make no mistake. Our kingdom is at war. Lack of awareness leaves us unprepared, not exempt. Spiritual reality transcends and continually influences the physical realm. Though our flesh cannot sense it, no greater reality exists than the spiritual and eternal. Divine heroines need to recognize the spiritual war raging around us at all times. We must equip ourselves with eternal armor to stand against the unseen enemy.

The concept of arming our souls is an ancient and biblical practice established upon this pressing need.

The earliest Christian warriors faced intense persecution and temptation. Despite suffering his own imprisonment, the Apostle Paul lamented more deeply the pressure and distractions threatening to crush these soldiers' faith. He crafted a list of defenses to equip them against the insidious enemy of their souls by using metaphors they understood.

> Put on the full armor of God, so that you can take your stand against the devil's schemes. For our struggle is not against flesh and blood, but against the rulers, against the authorities, against the powers of this dark world and against the spiritual forces of evil in the heavenly realms. Therefore put on the full armor of God,

so that when the day of evil comes, you may be able to stand your
ground, and after you have done everything, to stand.

—Ephesians 6:11–13

The apostle warned against false teachings, which tempted early
believers to trust in humanistic stage props like worldly knowledge.
Information which bolsters the ego instead of the soul offers all the spiritual defense of a cardboard weapon. He urged these ancient infantry
members to "be strong in the Lord and in his mighty power" (v. 10).
Like those who fought before us, we must learn to adopt the effective
defenses imparted to us by Christ and equip ourselves for battle.

Belt

Though a belt might seem inconsequential, Paul mentions it first in
his list of defenses. A soldier's belt served as more than an optional
accessory. Weapons, currency, ammunition, water, and food hung on
the leather strap holding a warrior's armor in place. Like this essential,
tying article of clothing, truth secures the other components of our
spiritual armor. We must remain honest with others, ourselves, and
God while dwelling in the truth of Scripture. A well-belted woman
submits herself to the Spirit's thought-detox daily.

Breastplate

Psalm 139:23–24 says, "Search me, God, and know my heart; test me
and know my anxious thoughts. See if there is any offensive way in
me, and lead me in the way everlasting." A princess warrior bears her
Lord's breastplate of righteousness. She grows in spiritual maturity,
developing more of Christ's character and nature throughout her
relationship to Him. But she doesn't depend on her own good behavior to protect her from evil. She must acknowledge her need to wear

the holiness of Jesus in order to guard her heart against all the sins affiliated with pride.

Boots

We women love shoes. We tend to pamper our toes with comfort, style, or both. Though the market's high-heeled fashions don't benefit our health, perhaps our attraction to footwear reflects the creator's design. As His heroines, we must fit our feet with readiness. Spiritual soles need to bear the ancient warrior's sharp cleats. The enemy will charge at each of us, whether or not we're ready. Circumstances will rattle our security. Slander will attack our identity. But a soul anchored in the peace of her salvation stands firm.

Shield

The lies and wounding blows shoot at us throughout this lifelong combat. As the ancient Romans soaked their shields, a cunning Christ-warrior drenches her faith in living water. We must raise our faith as our foremost defense against the "flaming arrows of the evil one" (Ephesians 6:16). As sisters in this fight, we are strongest when we raise our shields together. Emulating the tactics of early armies, we avoid fighting alone. Instead, we join in formation and use our shields to guard each other's vulnerable areas. If one heroine's faith falters, we step in to cover her against the foe.

Crown (or helmet, depending upon how you prefer to accessorize your heroine's garb)

Salvation must crown our identity and protect our mindsets. The prince of this world runs a relentless campaign to disconnect our soul and thoughts from centeredness upon God. Scripture warns us against the lure of other distracting focal points. "Do not conform to the pattern of this world, but be transformed by the renewing of your mind" (Romans 12:2). The helmet serves both to identify and guard a divine heroine.

Sword and Spear

While most of our armor defends us, Christ doesn't leave us without weapons. He modeled the use of both combat tools before commissioning them to us. First mentioned is "the sword of the Spirit, which is the word of God" (Ephesians 6:17). Jesus chose this means to defeat Satan while tempted in the desert. Ancient soldiers also carried a long-range spear,[19] which is not named in the list of armor but would have been familiar to the original readers and hearers of Paul's words in Ephesians. Paul might have intended the spear to correlate with our other weapon—prayer. "Pray in the Spirit on all occasions with all kinds of prayers and requests. With this in mind, be alert and always keep on praying for all the Lord's people" (v. 18). Paul cites the command to pray five times in four verses, boldly underscoring its value in spiritual warfare.

Connection as Our Greatest Artillery

Though connection isn't listed as part of the warrior's armor in Ephesians, other Scripture passages underscore its importance. Paul emphasized unity among believers a few chapters prior to the warfare passage (Ephesians 4:1–4) and alludes to the strengthening power of connecting with other believers in Christ, "From him the whole body, joined and held together by every supporting ligament, grows and builds itself up in love, as each part does its work" (v. 16).

---

19. David A. Kaden, "Roman Army" in The Lexham Bible Dictionary, eds. Edited by John D. Barry, David Bomar, Derek R. Brown, Rachel Klippenstein, Douglas Mangum, Carrie Sinclair Wolcott, Lazarus Wentz, Elliot Ritzema, and Wendy Widder (Bellingham, WA: Lexham Press, 2016).

When Paul wrote to the Corinthian church, he repeated this allegory to show the critical nature of our interconnected purpose as compared to the interdependence of a body's parts. "If one part suffers, every part suffers with it; if one part is honored, every part rejoices with it. Now you are the body of Christ, and each one of you is a part of it" (1 Corinthians 12:26–27).

Hebrews exhorts us to stick together and "spur one another on toward love and good deeds, not giving up meeting together, as some are in the habit of doing, but encouraging one another—and all the more as you see the Day approaching" (Hebrews 10:24–25).

Peter used the firm (and personal, recalling Jesus' identification of him in Matthew 16:18) imagery of stones to illustrate the potential of our united efforts, "You also, like living stones, are being built into a spiritual house to be a holy priesthood, offering spiritual sacrifices acceptable to God through Jesus Christ" (1 Peter 2:5).

Even among the moans of meaninglessness in the Book of Ecclesiastes, we find acknowledgement of the strengthening value of connectedness. "Two are better than one . . . If either of them falls down, one can help the other up. But pity anyone who falls and has no one to help them up. . . . Though one may be overpowered, two can defend themselves. A cord of three strands is not quickly broken" (Ecclesiastes 4:9–10, 12). Most poignant of all are the words of Jesus as He prayed to equip the body of believers through connection "that all of them may be one, Father, just as you are in me and I am in you. May they also be in us so that the world may believe that you have sent me. I have given them the glory that you gave me, that they may be one as we are one—I in them and you in me—so that they may be brought to complete unity. Then the world will know that you sent me and have loved them even as you have loved me" (John 17:21–23).

Scripture highlights our unity with Christ and one another as a vital source of strength toward fulfilling our purpose. Satan opposes fulfillment of God's will and therefore our unity. The enemy seeks to divide and weaken us, much the same way a lion will seek prey secluded from the herd. "Your enemy the devil prowls around like a roaring lion looking for someone to devour" (1 Peter 5:8).

A vicious nemesis plots against our sisters, scheming to cut us off from one another and our King. His deceptions attempt to rob women of their true heraldry. *But we do not have to buy into his lies.* "No, in all these things we are more than conquerors through him who loved us" (Romans 8:37).

The Lord has equipped us for battle and titled us for victory. Our true identity rests in Christ alone. If we stand in His name, we've already won the war.

A Heroine's Divine Armor

List the old patents of identity you must discard (e.g., self-slander, validation through means other than Christ).

_____

_____

_____

_____

Draw a coat of arms in the space below that establishes your identity as a heroic warrior in Christ. Feel free to use symbols to represent the features you listed in chapter ten's exercise.

Read Ephesians 6:10–18. Pray through the pieces of your spiritual armor. List specific ways you intend to improve your ability to wield each one.

Belt of Truth

_____

_____

_____

_____

Breastplate of Righteousness

_____

_____

_____

_____

Boots of Readiness

_____

_____

_____

_____

Shield of Faith

_____

_____

_____

_____

Helmet of Salvation

_____

_____

_____

_____

_____

Sword of the Spirit (Word of God)

_____

_____

_____

_____

_____

(Spear of) Prayer

_____

_____

_____

_____

_____

Empowerment Questions

1. What culture-based standards have you used to measure your self-worth?

_____

_____

_____

_____

_____

2. What impact could worldly measures of identity have upon our esteem?

_____

_____

_____

_____

_____

3. How do false sources of significance affect our purpose?

_____

_____

_____

_____

_____

4. Read Romans 8:16–17. How could this Scripture affect your self-image?

_____

_____

_____

_____

_____

5. What is one piece of spiritual armor you plan to fortify this week?

_____

_____

_____

_____

_____

Chapter 13

EXPERIENCING A HEROINE'S LOVE

Feeling unlovable remains a widespread struggle. Across generations and cultures, across the ages to the most distant history, the ache for soul-deep embrace defines the human experience. Many feel the symptoms of their deficiency but don't understand what's missing. Emptiness gnaws at the spine. Hunger stirs voracious bile into the gut, spurring an indefinable craving. A desperate binge to fill the growling void follows, grabbing for synthetics when true love eludes us. Until starvation of heart and soul wreaks havoc in our lives, we don't know we've poisoned ourselves with artificial additives.

Before I went to college, I believed my relationship with God was healthy. I assumed that daily prayer, Bible reading, and personal walks with the Lord guaranteed I was fine. Self-loathing and disconnection from others proved otherwise. Unhealthy priorities crowded Christ from the center of my heart. It never occurred to me that hating myself obstructed healthy relationships with God and others.

Genuine fulfillment comes from one source and one source only. You must stop searching around you and look up.

Despite attempts to mask my low self-esteem, spiritual anemia became more than obvious. Instead of walking with the Lord, insecurity usurped His place as my companion. Desperate for relationships with other people, a self-destructive paradigm poisoned my soul. God still loved me, but I crippled my ability to live in His love.

I clutched at toxic substitutes to fill the void. Crowds failed to quench the desert of loneliness. I opened my mouth wide for acceptance, longing to fill my empty soul with worth, but the world's sweet-tasting mirages turned to sand in my stomach. Spiritually, relationally, and personally starved, I counted rib bones through the skin of my soul. I saw nothing of substance between my hips and shoulders.

Praise God, before my heart failed altogether, He arrested my attention.

When I sank into earthly muck, Christ gathered a search party from across the heavens to draw me back into his heart. Despite my failure to listen, the Lord pursued me. He called me by name, beckoning over and over again. Jesus' voice reached like a shepherd's crook to rescue me from foolish wandering. His grace amazed me then, and it continues to amaze me today. I now strive to hear Him at the first whisper.

Perhaps your feet burn from wandering in emptiness. Maybe you've reached for acceptance, and the sting of rejection lashed your palms. Whether you are lost, wounded, or marooned in self-doubt, hope remains. The ulcerous hole in your starving core can be filled. You can experience satisfaction beyond all you ask or imagine. But genuine fulfillment comes from one source and one source only. You must stop searching *around* you and look *up*.

True love hovers just overhead. And He's dying to fill your parched heart until it overflows.

Ultimate Love Stories

The Lord so desired healing for His little ones that He laid aside His splendor and tucked Himself into a feeding trough. He exchanged heavenly surroundings for straw. Consider tossing aside every comfort and possession to live in squalor among people who will eventually malign and betray you. God the Father adored us enough to send His Son as a vulnerable infant into this brutal world.

God the Son loved us enough to come.

The King of kings birthed Himself into a displaced family facing national crisis. The oppressive government taxed people into starvation and forced overcrowding for a census so they could tax them even more. The world offered no accommodations for a carpenter, an outcast girl, or the newborn Lord. The only royal bling on the scene shimmered from a star, but its light halted outside the innkeeper's cave. This makeshift barn surrounded Mary's labor in stench and filth. After delivering Christ onto a pungent bed of hay, angels brought in unseemly visitors to celebrate—shepherds, the very men deemed unlovable by many surrounding ancient societies. Yet God chose them to meet the Messiah before the Magi had barely looked up and identified the strange star in the east.

The Christmas story illustrates true love so well and in so many ways. Our Father goes to amazing lengths to reach those mired in the sludge of rejection, emptiness, and hopelessness. He finds us when trudging through life's dust as though we don't belong anywhere and gently raises our chins to meet His loving gaze. He welcomes all those deemed unlovable by worldly standards: the scandalized teen, pungent laborers, and the blue-collar carpenter as A-list guests. Invitations go out to the well-educated and respectable guys too, but they're not seated ahead of the others. Jesus' impoverished birth demonstrates how God esteems us by our spiritual identity, not by our circumstances or physical appearance.

First John 4:10 sums up God's adoration for us. "This is love: not that we loved God, but that he loved us and sent his Son as an atoning sacrifice for our sins."

The Christmas story culminates with the ultimate love story at Easter. Not only did the Son of God lay aside His royal crown and resplendent heavenly dwelling to visit us, He also endured intense suffering to save us. Romans specialized in torture. In fact, the word *excruciating* entered our vocabulary because no existing word captured the pain of crucifixion.

In addition to this indescribable pain, Jesus suffered emotional and spiritual affliction. Each time one of God's children betrayed Him, turned her back, disobeyed, or rebelled—every sin from the past and every sin from the future—burdened His battered heart. His breathing and shoulders labored under the weight of all we did or would do in the name of sin. Yet Jesus let the offenses die with His agony. Afterward, friends took Christ's battered and oozing flesh and swaddled it, much as His mother had after His birth. Then they laid His cold body inside another cave.

But the world's evil brutality, with all its rejection, betrayal, and savage wounding, proved unable to destroy love. Even death could not end the ultimate love story. Our Hero came back even stronger. And when Jesus rose, He paved the way for us to experience intimacy with God forever. Anyone who chose to love Him would never have to live as an unlovable soul again. No more death. And no more emotional cave-dwelling.

Jesus draws us close to His heart as He carries us into divine relationship. With love beyond our imagination, Jesus embraces our souls. He lifts us up before the Father, where God drenches us with blessings. Dwelling in eternal love begins *right now*.

Not after we die.

Christmas and Easter show how Jesus sacrificed Himself to open our pathway. He came to us, died, and then rose so we could come to Him, die to self, rise, and live fulfilled. The Son of God extends His nail-scarred hands, and in doing so, invites us to dwell in His Father's heart forever. As soon as we accept Christ's embrace, we rise from our earthly origins to live in the resplendent kingdom of God's presence as His children.

Perfect Restoration

A canyon might loom between where you stand and the joy of fulfillment. Toes gripping the cliff-edge of knowledge, you gaze across the vast gap. Feeling lovable remains an impassible leap away. Vultures circle in the glaring distance between your head and heart. How do you vault from knowing about love to immersing your soul in it?

Experience bridges the void between emotion and reasoning. Anchored on the truth, you can engineer footers and support beams in your lifestyle to bring love's words into your spirit. Strategic activities create a framework for walking in intimacy with love incarnate. Building environmental and mental structures to cultivate God-esteem prepares your spirit to experience true acceptance.

But how to accomplish this? Start by optimizing your input and influence. While nutritionists emphasize the old adage that says, "You are what you eat," what you take into your mind and spirit carries far more power to change your life. Negative messages flood our eyes and ears daily. Advertisements insist we're deficient. Culture pressures us to pursue their acceptance. Buy into the anxiety. Conform to the worship of earth's standards. Human nature tends to default toward nonspiritual mindsets, so you must plan ways to remain connected with God's presence. Intentionally place reminders of how much God loves you in your daily environment. You can start with the Scripture passages listed in this book. Write them on sticky notes, then place them on your walls, mirror, fridge, calendar, phone, dashboard, computer—anywhere you may see them. Change them up at least once a week so you don't grow blind to their influence.

Get around people who will pray with and for you. Surround yourself with God's love wrapped in skin. Sorrows impede spiritual experiences at times, making it tough to dwell in or feel Jesus' love.

The Lord designed us for human relationships. Not so we would expect people to meet our needs. They can't. Human beings cannot esteem your personality or fill your empty heart and soul. God alone supplies our needs. But He knows tangible beings experience love best with hugs. Because of that, He engineered vessels to carry His blessings to us when we're struggling to focus on the Lord's presence.

Art bypasses the mind's rejection setting. Filling your world with divine inspiration cultivates an environment primed for experiencing intimacy with Jesus. Keeping that in mind, flood your home, car, and workspace with spiritually uplifting music. Dance through chores. Soak in faith-spurring stories.

Then . . . get out. In nature, I mean. Prayerful connection with the majesty of Creation immerses us in the wonder of His love. Meditate upon the details He brushed into the masterpiece of the universe. God had no reason to invent celestial landscapes, gardens, or animals for Himself. The Father imagined the whole project as a dwelling to enrapture our senses.

Participate with God in celebrating His loving presence. Carve into your schedule meal times, study discussion times, play times, and worship times with Jesus. Use tangible cues and techniques to enhance your awareness of His presence. Mark your calendar until the habit of spending time with God secures itself in your life.

Lay yourself in the Creator's hands and ask Him to shape you into a conduit. Absorb grace. Give grace. Listen for Christ's prompts throughout each day. I've heard them in the grocery store as often as at church. Look for God's love in the eyes of those who need it. Don't overlook discovering it in those who seem least likely to reflect it. Allowing love to lead your conversations, encourage others to dwell in Christ's love. Be a blessing every day throughout the day. Don't allow fear to inhibit you. Reaching out and getting your hands dirty offers the best opportunity to watch things grow.

Inhabiting the Heart of God

Imagine crawling into the heart of God. Love pulses all around you—its rhythm echoing through your senses. His heartbeat loosens the veil from your eyes, and for the first time you realize who you are. Nestled in His warmth, aches dissolve. Worry dissipates like fog introduced to the sun's glory. Truth floods your mind, uprooting lies and sweeping them away in its healing flow. Injured soul-parts regenerate. Trust strengthens, deepens. The handprint of a child He adores hangs on the inner walls of His heart—and it is yours.

The haven of God's love empowers and inspires. Compassion incubates in the security of perfect acceptance. From within the Lord's heart, our arms naturally reach toward others. Our hands grow warm. Fingers and toes tingle, searching for a way to share divine love. Jesus directs loving hands and feet by opening our eyes. His grace radiates through, removing judgmental views from the inside out.

The Lord cherishes us. We are His babies, even as we age. His fingers reach out toward tender toes, longing to hold our soles in His palm. He dreams of caressing His little one's cheek to evoke a smile. God reflects upon the joy with which He formed you—taking time to add a curl or adjust the hue of your eyes. The ridges of each fingertip were sculpted by love.

Immerse yourself in *His* perspective. Allow God to infuse every dimension of your life with purifying love. This one "thing" in my life has allowed the Lord's essence to flood my awareness, deepening my intimacy with Him. I see, hear, and speak differently from within the Lord's heart. As a counselor, I've stepped into the Lord's heart and allowed His Spirit to pour through me. Prostitutes, addicts, and abuse victims glimmer before me, precious gems in the eyes of Christ. Wealthy and poor clients share one resource of grace and truth and receive equal adoration from one Father.

I invite you to crawl with me into the heart of God. Take this opportunity to transform your attitudes toward God, toward self, and toward others. Inhabiting God's heart soaks our relationships with the Lord, ourselves, and others in a healing bath.

Divine Love's Imprint

On a sheet of paper, trace your hand and include part of your wrist in the drawing. Notice the imperfections in the outline. Recall any obstacles to believing you are worthy of God's love. Draw a circle on the wrist segment of your picture and write your "unlovable" thoughts inside the circle. Now, sketch a spike pointing to the circle. On or beside the spike, write out John 3:16 and Romans 5:8. Use a red marker to blot out the circle.

Now, regard the outline of your hand. Write above the fingers, "For my Father, the Lord of lord and King of kings." Choose the Scripture passages most meaningful to you from the Who I Am list from pages 64–71, and write them on the fingers and palm.

Place your hand on the imprint and pray about dedicating your actions and identity to serve as the divine heroine Christ has called you to become in the kingdom of God.

Empowerment Questions

1. Consider the stories of Christmas and Easter in light of John 4:10. How might these truths renew your attitude about your identity?

_____

_____

_____

_____

_____

2. Write a note of gratitude to God for His restorative love, making all hearts sufficient.

_____

_____

_____

_____

_____

3. Does inadequacy continue to plague your sense of identity? If your struggle seems overwhelming or too difficult to manage alone, consult a pastor, life coach, or therapist.

_____

_____

_____

_____

4. How might you optimize your input and influence?

_____

_____

_____

_____

_____

_____

5. What next steps do you plan to take after reading this book?

_____

_____

_____

_____

_____

_____

CONCLUSION

YOU: REDEFINED, LOVABLE, BE-YOU-TIFUL

Redefined

Being redefined means defining yourself according to your relationship with God and seeing your calling as a journey of commitment and not a mere checklist of results (see Hebrews 11:39). It means realizing He has given you a purpose, not perfection. It means knowing He desires intimacy, not busyness (see John 17:20–24).

Being redefined means being present with God, listening *and* receptive to what you hear Him say (see 1 Corinthians 2:9–12). Being patient with His work in and through you.

A redefined woman stands shoulder-to-shoulder with all the divinely renamed heroes of eternity. Abram, remade into Abraham, the father of nations. Sarai, renewed as Sarah, God's princess. Jacob promoted to Israel. Simon, redeemed as Peter, "the rock."

"This means that anyone who belongs to Christ has become a new person. The old life is gone; a new life has begun (2 Corinthians 5:17). The redefined woman no longer settles for the name assuming her mortal status but instead answers to her title as a joint heir with Christ. Engraved by God's skillful hand, her spiritual armor bears His crest. She wears a new identity no human hand can unwrite.

Becoming redefined is about transformation, not arrival. "We all, with unveiled faces, are looking as in a mirror at the glory of the Lord and are being transformed into the same image from glory to glory; this is from the Lord who is the Spirit" (2 Corinthians 3:18 HCSB). Our divine redefinition is about the odyssey, not the destination.

Lovable

What makes us lovable? The one who created us, by definition, creates lovable children in His image. "The Spirit himself testifies with our spirit that we are God's children" (Romans 8:16). As the old saying goes, "God doesn't make junk."

It's important to remember this, especially when you're feeling unlovable. Keep concrete examples in mind. Like . . . babies.

Have you noticed that newborns don't do anything but sleep and dirty their diapers? Of course there is the occasional bad temper. Through their tantrums they demand changing or feeding or holding. Some are even odd-featured, without the plump characteristics of an Anne Geddes portrait. Yet all infants are lovable because they were created with an indelible beauty. The world has not yet hidden their divine fingerprints under labels or convinced them to discard their charming Christ-dimples. We see the essence of potential sparkling in their tiny eyes. Maturation can bury God's impressions, but when we look closely, we see the potential He carves into us cannot and does not vanish.

I know because if I gaze upon *my* grown child's face, I still see my baby's features.

> For you created my inmost being; you knit me together in
> my mother's womb. I praise you because I am fearfully and

wonderfully made; your works are wonderful, I know that
full well.

—Psalm 139:13–14

Be-YOU-tiful

Look into the mirror. See your inborn self, the one God sees because
it's the one He created. God crafted unique blessings into *your* life, *your*
personality, *your* spirit. Some were woven into your soul before birth.
Others He sprinkled in as an added bonus as you grew from infant to
toddler. From toddler to young child. From young child to adolescent.
From adolescent to woman.

Though you might feel as though you have little or no value, you
cannot be less significant than God's other children (or more worthy
on our own merit). This might sound obvious to some. Ephesians 2
confirms this, as well as countless other verses, but depression and
despair slither into our minds and hiss all sorts of things that seem to
make sense in the silence. But speak them aloud and they only sound
ridiculous. Kind of like turning on the light to dispense the vermin.

Trust me; exposing this common, "I'm the most worthless" lie by
writing it out or speaking it before an advisor robs half its power. The
other half shrivels under the blaze of truth. Every. Life. Matters. *Every*
individual has unique significance to God . . . or *no one* has it. If you
are of no value, neither is anyone else.

Remember this above all else—by defining God as good and perfect,
we also declare His creation has worth. Yes, including you.

Especially you.

Christ emphasized compassion throughout His ministry, culmi-
nating the lesson as He stretched out His arms on the Cross in the
ultimate display of love. Jesus implored us to love those who God

loves, and in doing so *we show our love for God*. He expanded the definition of God's children so the command to love no longer excluded anyone.

At the culmination of His earthly ministry, Jesus' final breath declared, "It is finished" (John 19:30). His perfect sacrifice made it possible for us to draw into the presence of divine love, for "At that moment the curtain of the temple was torn in two from top to bottom" (Matthew 27:51). This moment was significant because "the curtain divided people from the place where God had localized His presence. The tearing from top to bottom (Matthew 27:51) symbolized the fact that now, because of Jesus' death, people had freer access to God as they no longer had to go through the sacrificial system (cf. Romans 5:2; Ephesians 2:18; 3:12). Jesus was the only Sacrifice needed to enable people to have a proper relationship with God."[20]

Through Christ, believers can now enjoy the embrace of God as Father. As the author of Hebrews assured early Christians, "Therefore, brothers and sisters, since we have confidence to enter the Most Holy Place by the blood of Jesus, by a new and living way opened for us through the curtain, that is, his body, and since we have a great priest over the house of God, let us draw near to God with a sincere heart and with the full assurance that faith brings" (Hebrews 10:19–22).

The torn veil also draws the Father's children together, as it "signified the uniting of Jew and Gentile, by the removing of the partition wall between them, which was the ceremonial law, by which the Jews were distinguished from all other people . . . Christ died, to rend all dividing veils, and to make all his one."[21]

---

20. John A. Martin "Luke," in *The Bible Knowledge Commentary: An Exposition of the Scriptures,* eds. J. F. Walvoord and R. B. Zuck. (Wheaton, IL: Victor Books, 1995).

21. Matthew Henry, *Matthew Henry's Commentary on the Whole Bible: Complete and Unabridged in One Volume* (Peabody: Hendrickson, 1994).

On the eve of His Crucifixion, Jesus prayed for us to share the intimacy of God's glory (John 17:22–23). He received God's glory and love and then imparted them to us. Jesus's prayer shows His heartfelt desire for us to operate in perfect relational balance—to receive glory through God-esteem, to dwell in intimate fellowship with the Lord, and to share Christ's love with others.

Links to self, God, and others correlate like waterworks. Conduits must be sturdy, open to the source, and free from pollutants. Any lack of these disables the waterway. Personal, spiritual, and interpersonal health unlock the floodgates of joy. Truth, love, and healing surge unhindered along a clear and sturdy viaduct. Blessings spill over our edges onto thirsty bystanders. Understanding who we are and *whose* we are illuminates fountains along those viaducts. Living water energizes each spout through which it flows. Jesus said, "Whoever drinks the water I give them will never thirst. Indeed, the water I give them will become in them a spring of water welling up to eternal life" (John 4:14).

The Word (Jesus himself) created you. You. He is the only one with the authority to define and redefine who you are.

In many cultures, one's name is synonymous with one's identity. When Moses asked God to reveal His name, God said, "I AM WHO I AM" (Exodus 3:14). His answer implied that man could neither grasp the entirety of His nature nor begin to have authority over His power. YHWH, or Yahweh, as the name "I AM" was probably pronounced, became known as a God in relationship to His people. The Great I AM was not named by His people, but instead He often named His servants. Yahweh called Moses a leader when he was still a murderer in exile. He called timid Gideon out of the threshing floor as a mighty warrior before Gideon believed who he was destined to become. Jesus addressed an adulteress with a term of respect while she still lay in the dust at His feet. Simon was renamed as a rock before he was refined and set into a leadership role.

In the biblical account of the birth of King Solomon, the words found in 2 Samuel are quite clear as to how God felt about this precious life.

> Then David comforted his wife Bathsheba, and he went to her and made love to her. She gave birth to a son, and they named him Solomon. The LORD loved him; and because the LORD loved him, he sent word through Nathan the prophet to name him Jedidiah.
>
> —2 Samuel 12:24–25

Jedidiah means "loved by the Lord."

Like Solomon, you and I are defined by the name *God* gives us. We are not defined by who we have been in the past. I am more than who I was and you are more than who you were when we believed the lies. What's more, I am more than who I believe I can be right now. And you are more than you believe you can be right now.

We are who the Great "I AM" says we are.

That's the truth.

What will you do then? Believe the lies of one who cares nothing about you . . . or believe the word of the one who created you in His image? In His perfection? The one who loves you enough to have sent His Son with the express purpose of stopping all the lies Satan ever hissed into the ears of God's children?

He has called you by a great name. He has called you *lovable*.

Write that on your "hello my name is" sticker. Press it against your heart. As a heroine of divine esteem for your sisters, wear it proudly!

ADDITIONAL CONTENT

Visit www.tinayeager.com/beautifulwarrior for videos to complement each chapter. Request a downloadable leader guide for group study.

I'm also available to speak to your organization in person. I'd love to meet your group and offer you encouragement along your spiritual journey and may be able to tailor material for the needs of your participants. Submit a request on the contact page of tinayeager.com, and we'll be in touch soon.

RESOURCE LIST

The following resources might inspire your next steps as a divine heroine. The utmost sources of inspiration and strength are the Holy Spirit and participation in a healthy, local church family. If the message in these pages has stirred trauma or other deep issues in your heart, mind, and soul, please reach out for support from a counseling pastor or licensed professional therapist.

Counseling and Life-Coaching Resources
Crisis Text Line—Text NAMI to 741-741
National Sexual Assault Hotline—Call 800-656-HOPE (4673)
National Domestic Violence Hotline—Call 800-799-SAFE (7233)
National Suicide Prevention Lifeline—Call 800-273-TALK (8255)
Please call 9-1-1 if there is an imminent risk of harm.
Christian Care Connect—provides a listing of local therapists: https://connect.aacc.net/?search_type=distance
Christian Coaches Network International—provides a listing of Christian life coaches: https://christiancoaches.com/find-a-coach/
National Alliance on Mental Illness (NAMI)—support for those with mental illness diagnoses and their families, including local support groups, programs, advocacy, and a national helpline to answer questions at 1-800-950-NAMI (6264) or www.nami.org

Anxiety and Depression Association of America—provides resources, support, tips, and a listing of therapists: https://adaa.org/finding-help

Support for Financial or Domestic Violence Issues
Live Your Dream—educational grants and domestic violence programs: http://www.liveyourdream.org/get-help/index.html
Need Help Paying Bills—connects people with local financial assistance programs: www.needhelppayingbills.com
Legal Services Corporation—legal assistance for low-income Americans: www.lsc.gov
YWCA—Domestic violence services, women's health programs, racial justice, job training and empowerment, financial literacy, early childhood development, STEM programs for girls, academic scholarships: Find your local YWCA at www.ywca.org
World YWCA Violence Against Women Fact Sheet: http://www.worldywca.org/wp-content/uploads/2016/11/Violence-against-women-fact-sheet.pdf

Faith-Based Women's Organizations and Online Inspirational Content
Christian Women in Media Association—Resources for women in media-related ministries: https://cwima.org/category/cwima-blog/
The Association of Junior Leagues International—Blog articles on self-esteem for women: https://www.ajli.org/?nd=p-do-comm-ip-self-esteem
The Association of Junior Leagues International—Blog articles on women's health: https://www.ajli.org/?nd=p-do-comm-ip-womens-health
National Association of Christian Women in Business—membership and articles to support business women: http://nacwib.com/blog/

National Association of Christian Women Entrepreneurs—free online trainings, blogs, and membership opportunities: https://nacwe.org /courses/freetraining/

Proverbs 31 Ministries—blog articles, devotions, and ministry training: www.proverbs31.org

Today's Christian Woman—articles addressing women's issues: www .todayschristianwoman.com/topics/church-life-ministry/womens -ministry

**If you enjoyed this book, will you consider sharing
the message with others?**

Let us know your thoughts at info@newhopepublishers.com.
You can also let the author know by visiting or sharing a photo
of the cover on our social media pages or leaving a review
at a retailer's site. All of it helps us get the message out!

Twitter.com/NewHopeBooks

Facebook.com/NewHopePublishers

Instagram.com/NewHopePublishers

———————

New Hope® Publishers is an imprint of Iron Stream Media,
which derives its name from Proverbs 27:17,
"As iron sharpens iron, so one person sharpens another."

This sharpening describes the process of discipleship,
one to another. With this in mind, Iron Stream Media provides
a variety of solutions for churches, missionaries, and nonprofits ranging
from in-depth Bible study curriculum and Christian book publishing
to custom publishing and consultative services. Through the popular
Life Bible Study and Student Life Bible Study brands, ISM provides
web-based full-year and short-term Bible study teaching plans
as well as printed devotionals, Bibles, and discipleship curriculum.

For more information on ISM and New Hope Publishers, please visit

IronStreamMedia.com

NewHopePublishers.com